... Repertory Theatre Company
... co-production with
the Edinburgh International Festival
presents

the world premiere of

Prayer Room

by Shan Khan

commissioned by the
Edinburgh International Festival

First previewed on 17 Aug 2005
at Birmingham Repertory Theatre

Premiered on 22 Aug 2005 at the
Edinburgh International Festival

Birmingham Repertory Theatre
Centenary Square
Broad Street
Birmingham
B1 2EP

www.birmingham-rep.co.uk.

Birmingham Repertory Theatre Company in co-production with the Edinburgh International Festival presents

Prayer Room

by Shan Khan

Fiz Riz Ahmed

Bunce Jimmy Akingbola

Brother Kazi Tolga Safer

Griffin William Ellis

Rilla Hannah Watkins

Jade Ashley Madekwe

Reuben Iddo Goldberg

Brother Convert
Peter Swander

Principal Howard Ward

Director Angus Jackson

Designer Lucy Osborne

Lighting Designer Neil Austin

Composer Alex Gallafent

Casting Director
Julia Horan CDG

Fight Director Terry King

Assistant Lighting Designer
Fiona Simpson

With thanks to all the staff at
Birmingham Repertory Theatre

With thanks to Nicola from
Birmingham Drugline
(Helpline 0121 632 6363)

Stage Manager Liz Crossan

Deputy Stage Manager
Joolz Clough

Assistant Stage Manager
Laura Ainsworth

The Cast

Fiz
Riz Ahmed

Riz trained at Oxford University and graduated from Central School Of Speech And Drama this year.

Theatre credits include: *Julius Caesar* (Thelma Holt Japan tour 2004); *The Beauty Of Things* (Hampstead Theatre) and *The Wedge* (Network Theatre/Floodtide Theatre).

Film includes: *The Road To Guantanamo* directed by Michael Winterbottom, *Got Soul* and *Empty Rhetoric*.

Riz is a professional MC and lead vocalist for up and coming drum 'n' bass band The Confidential Collective. He has recently won the Bombay Bronx and the One Music/Battlescars MC battle tournaments.

Bunce
Jimmy Akingbola

Jimmy trained at the Academy Of Live And Recorded Arts

Theatre credits include: *Blue/Orange* (Sheffield Crucible and tour); *People Next Door* (Traverse Edinburgh/ Stratford East); *Playing Fields* (Soho Theatre); *Thumbelina* (Stephen Joseph Theatre); *Naked Justice* (West Yorkshire Playhouse and tour); *Baby Doll* (National Theatre/Albery); *The Changeling* (National Theatre); *Nativity, The Shooky* and *Behzti* (Birmingham Repertory Theatre); *The Ramayana* (National Theatre/ Birmingham Repertory Theatre) and *Ready Or Not Raw* (Theatre Royal Stratford East).

Television includes: *Blackbeard, The Royal, Who Killed PC Blakelock, The Crouches, Stupid, Roger Roger, Doctors, The Slightly Filthy Show* and *The South Bank Show*.

Radio includes: *Ibadan, Troilus And Cressida, The Fire Children, A Noise In The Night, Clothes Of Nakedness, Westway, Trinidad Sisters* and *Dancing Backwards*.

Film includes: *Anansi* and *The Car*.

Griffin
William Ellis

William graduated from LAMDA in July this year, and *Prayer Room* is his first professional engagement.

Jade
Ashley Madekwe

Ashley graduated from RADA this year, having left early to appear in *Little Sweet Thing* (Hampstead Theatre/tour). Prior to training, credits included:

Television: *Teachers*, *Hope And Glory* and *The Bill*.

Film: *Storm Damage*

Radio: *Far From Home* and *Tell Tale*.

Reuben
Iddo Goldberg

Recent film credits include: *I Could Never Be Your Woman*, *No Snow*, *Little Trip To Heaven*, *Match Point*, *Suzie Gold*, *Pot Luck* and *Uprising*.

Recent television credits include: *The Last Rights*, *Nathan Barley*, *Little Britain* and *Attachments*.

This is Iddo's first professional theatre engagement.

The Cast

Brother Kazi
Tolga Safer

Tolga trained at Mountview.

Theatre credits include: *Venezuela* and *Bintou* (Arcola Theatre).

Television includes: *Casualty* and *She's Gone*.

Film includes: *Harry Potter And The Goblet Of Fire*, *Get The Picture*, *Culture Menace*, *Turkish Coffee* and *Chain Gangs*.

Brother Convert
Peter Swander

Peter trained at Guildhall School of Music and Drama and at Vakhtangov Theatre School, Moscow.

Theatre credits include: *When Harry Met Sally* (Theatre Royal Haymarket).

Film includes: *The Painter* and *The Tiger And The Snow*.

Radio includes: *Death At The Desert Inn*.

Principal
Howard Ward

Rilla
Hannah Watkins

Theatre credits include: *Incomplete And Random Acts Of Kindness* (Royal Court); *Spring Awakening* (Young Vic); *Six Degrees Of Separation* (Manchester Royal Exchange); *Night Owls* and *A Day In Dull Armour* (Royal Court); *The Good Hope* (National Theatre); *Neville's Island* (Palace Theatre Watford); *The Mysteries, Johnny On The Spot, Wind In The Willows, Mountain Giants* and *Night Of The Iguana* (National Theatre); *All's Well That Ends Well, As You Like It, The Two Noble Kinsmen, The Fair Maid Of The West, The Balcony* and *Speculators* (RSC); *Faith, Attempts On Her Life* and *Pale Horse* (Royal Court).

Television and film includes: *Cash Back, Ghost Squad, Heartbeat, The Government Inspector, Doctors, Crisis Command, Family Affairs, Absolute Power, Amnesia, Murder Investigation Team, Unconditional Love, The Bill, Holby City, Inspector Lynley Mysteries, Gypsy Girl, Burnside, Doctors, The Bill, This Is Personal, Dream Team, Insiders, EastEnders, Story Store, Jake's Progress, Peak Practice, Between The Lines* and *London's Burning*. Radio includes: *Beware Of The Trains* and *Let's Move*

Direction icludes: *The Sociable Plover* (Old Red Lion); *The Taxman* (Radio 4 – Sony nominated) and *The Last Dare* (Radio 4).

Hannah trained at Central School Of Speech And Drama.

Theatre credits include: *Harry In The Moonlight* (Northcott Theatre Exeter); *Vincent In Brixton* (Manchester Library Theatre); *Be My Baby* (Salisbury Theatre); *The Adding Machine* (Rogue State); *Descent* (Birmingham Repertory Theatre); *Camera Obscura* (Almeida); *The Magic Toyshop* (Shared Experience/ tour); *Frankenstein* and *Mother Clap's Molly House* (National Theatre studio); *Remembrance Of Things Past* and *Romeo And Juliet* (National Theatre); *Six Degrees Of Separation* (Sheffield Crucible) and *The Lion The Witch And The Wardrobe* (RSC).

Television and film includes: *Puritan, Holby City, Sylvia, The Late Twentieth, Fall Of The House Of Usher* and *The People Are The Forest*.

Radio includes: *The Frederika Quartet* and *Thea's Diaries*.

The Creative Team

Shan Khan
Author

Shan Khan won the Verity Bargate Award in 2000, for his first stage-play *Office*, which received its World Premiere at the Edinburgh International Festival 2001, before transferring to the Soho Theatre London and Teatro Belli Rome. In 2003 he was BAFTA-nominated for the short film *Candy Bar Kid* which he wrote and directed. He has written various TV Drama and Film for BBC, ITV and Channel 4, including *The Vice*, *River City* and BBC One Afternoon Plays.

He has recently completed his second short-film, *Shop Window*, with aid from Screen Yorkshire; is preparing to shoot his first Feature-Film, *Battersea Park* in 2006; is developing original drama-series for Channel 4 and BBC ; and is writing the libretto for *Gaddafi The Opera*, with the English National Opera, music by Asian Dub Foundation, for September 2006.

He can't ski yet, but plans to learn how next year.

Angus Jackson
Director

Directing credits include: *Elmina's Kitchen* by Kwame Kwei-Armah (tour and West End); *Fix Up* by Kwame Kwei-Armah (National Theatre); *Fuddy Meers* by David Lindsay-Abaire (Birmingham Repertory Theatre/West End); *Elmina's Kitchen* (National Theatre); *Dealer's Choice* by Patrick Marber and *My Night With Reg* by Kevin Elyot (Birmingham Repertory Theatre); *Sexual Perversity In Chicago* and *The Shawl* both by David Mamet (Sheffield Crucible). He has also directed for the *24 Hour Plays* at The Old Vic and on Broadway. He filmed *Elmina's Kitchen* for BBC4, for which he was nominated for a BAFTA, and recently completed his first short film *Old Street*, written by Patrick Marber. He was educated at King Edward's School, Birmingham.

Lucy Osborne
Designer

Lucy Osborne's recent theatre credits include: *The Unthinkable* by Steve Waters (Sheffield Theatres) and *The Suppliants* (Battersea Arts Centre). She was a participant on the Young Vic Shorts project *Love and Money* by Dennis Kelly. Other work includes *Generation* (Gate Theatre, London) and the Hotbed Festival of New Writing which included *Butterfly Fingers* by Fraser Grace, *Gaugleprixtown* by Andrew Muir and *Changed So Much I Thought I Knew You* by Steve Waters (venues throughout Cambridge and Latchmere Theatre, London). Forthcoming projects include *The Long, The Short And The Tall* (Sheffield Lyceum and tour).

Lucy is also the venue designer and a technical advisor to the National Student Drama Festival.

Neil Austin
Lighting Designer

Theatre includes: Henry IV pts.1&2, Fix Up, A Prayer For Owen Meany, Further Than The Furthest Thing, The Night Season and The Walls (National Theatre); Julius Caesar and Two Gentlemen Of Verona (Royal Shakespeare Company); Caligula, After Miss Julie, Henry IV, World Music and The Cosmonaut's Last Message... (Donmar Warehouse); Macbeth and Romance (Almeida); Flesh Wound and Trust (Royal Court); Japes (Theatre Royal, Haymarket); A Life In The Theatre (Apollo, West End); On The Ceiling (Birmingham Repertory Theatre & West End); Fuddy Meers (Birmingham Repertory Theatre & West End); Cuckoos (BITE, Barbican). Neil has also designed the lighting for many productions at: Sheffield Crucible, The Royal Exchange, Manchester, West Yorkshire Playhouse, Bristol Old Vic, Royal Theatre, Northampton, Liverpool Playhouse, Traverse Edinburgh as well as internationally.

Dance includes: Rhapsody (Royal Ballet, Royal Opera House); The Soldier's Tale (ROH2, Linbury Theatre); Darkness And Light (Orchard Hall Theatre, Tokyo & Expo Dome, Nagoya).

Opera includes: The Cricket Recovers, Man And Boy: Dada and The Embalmer (Almeida Opera); Chorus! (Welsh National Opera); L'Orfeo (Opera City, Tokyo) and Pulse Shadows (Queen Elizabeth Hall).

Musicals include: Jekyll And Hyde (UK Tour); Babes In Arms (I.F.M.T) and Spend, Spend, Spend (UK Tour).

Alex Gallafent
Composer

Scores include: Fuddy Meers (Birmingham Repertory Theatre / West End); Late One Night (short film); Sexual Perversity In Chicago / The Shawl (Crucible, Sheffield); Dealer's Choice (Theatr Clwyd); Body And Soul (Gatehouse) and The Circle (Oxford Stage Co). Alex read philosophy & theology at Oxford before training as an actor at LAMDA: his work includes performances for the Tokyo Globe, English National Opera, Bolton Octagon and the Old Vic. Alex is also a radio producer for the BBC.

Fiona Simpson
Assistant Lighting Designer

Fiona trained at LAMDA. Her first lighting designs were at the New Wolsey Theatre Ipswich, and included Arcadia, The Devil's Cardinal and Noel And Gertie. She started freelance work in 1997 and worked with Eastern Angles Theatre Company Ipswich, lighting two shows as well as a number of national tours. She has also worked on Almeida Theatre shows; Judas Kiss and Naked at The Playhouse and The Iceman Cometh (Old Vic). In 1999 she worked at the Old Vic on Amadeus and Jeffrey Bernard Is Unwell, which was also filmed for television. Other work includes: I Am Who I Am, Day Of The Triffids and Turn Of The Screw (New Wolsey Theatre Ipswich); work for The Oxford Drama School in Oxford and London, Southwark Playhouse and Eastern Angles, as well as working as Associate Lighting Designer for Jean Kalman, relighting Festen at The Lyric Shaftesbury Avenue, and assisting him on By The Bog Of Cats at The Wyndhams.

THE REP

Birmingham Repertory Theatre

Birmingham Repertory Theatre is one of Britain's leading national theatre companies. From its base in Birmingham, The REP produces over twenty new productions each year.

The commissioning and production of new work lies at the core of The REP's programme. In 1998 the company launched The Door, a venue dedicated to the production and presentation of new work. This, together with an investment in commissioning new drama from some of Britain's brightest and best writing talent, gives The REP a unique position in British theatre. Indeed, through the extensive commissioning of new work The REP is providing vital opportunities for the young and emerging writing talent that will lead the way in the theatre of the future. The forthcoming Autumn season includes Shan Khan's *Prayer Room* in co-production with the Edinburgh International Festival alongside new plays from Peter Quilter (*Glorious*), Jess Walters (*Promises And Lies*), Tamsin Oglesby (*Only The Lonely*) and Deborah Gearing (*Rosalind: A Question of Life*).

REP productions regularly transfer to London and also tour nationally and internationally. Over the last few years several productions have been seen in London including *Of Mice And Men*, *The Birthday Party* and *The Old Masters*, with *The Snowman* running at The Peacock theatre for seven consecutive years.

Artistic Director **Jonathan Church**
Executive Director **Stuart Rogers**
Associate Director (Literary) **Ben Payne**

Box Office 0121 236 4455
Book online at www.birmingham-rep.co.uk

EUROPEAN COMMUNITY

European Regional
Development Fund

EDINBURGH INTERNATIONAL FESTIVAL

The Edinburgh International Festival was established in 1947. Long ranked as one of the most important cultural celebrations in the world, from the beginning the Festival has presented programmes of classical music, opera, theatre and dance of the highest possible standard, involving the best artists in the world. Founders of the Festival include Rudolf Bing, then the General Manager of Glyndebourne Opera, Henry Harvey Wood, the Head of the British Council in Scotland, and a group of civic leaders from the City of Edinburgh. They believed that the Festival should enliven and enrich the cultural life of Europe, Britain and Scotland and 'provide a platform for the flowering of the human spirit'. They also recognised that, if the Festival succeeded in its artistic ambitions, it would create a major new source of tourism revenue for Edinburgh and for Scotland. These founding principles are as relevant today as they were nearly 60 years ago.

The Edinburgh International Festival is programmed by its Director, currently Sir Brian McMaster. Artists perform at the Festival at the Director's invitation, with the Festival administration being responsible for all aspects of the promotion and management of its events.

Box Office 0131 473 2000
Book online at www.eif.co.uk

Scottish
Arts Council

·EDINBVRGH·
THE CITY OF EDINBURGH COUNCIL

Prayer Room
Shan Khan

ff

faber and faber

First published in 2005
by Faber and Faber Limited
3 Queen Square London WC1N 3AU

Typeset by Country Setting, Kingsdown, Kent CT14 8ES
Printed in England by Intype Libra Ltd

A CIP record for this book
is available from the British Library

ISBN 0–571–23107–1

2 4 6 8 10 9 7 5 3 1

For my Father

God bless you Dad

Love and blessings also

My mum, brothers, sisters, nephews and niece, Marsali,
Evie, Allan, Toto, Eduardo, Irvy and Annie, Paul and Cindy,
Bash, Sue, Kip, Katie, Fay and all at The Agency, Angus J,
Julia, Al P, Simon C, Hayles, Jared, Kaare, Mairi, Avin,
Mark T, Fi, Janey, Antonia B, Steve and ADF, Alan C,
Angus B, Dan D, Chris R, Graeme, Joycie, Riley, James R,
Malachy, Sidra, Henry A-J, Tim G, The Weaver, Tony C,
Jonathan and all at the Birmingham Rep, Brian,
Susie and all at the Edinburgh International Festival,
all the cast, crew, audience, Dinah and all at Faber –
and for all the coffees George, Carmela, Paulo,
Mustapha and Miguel.

CHARACTERS

Fiz
Bunce
Brother Kazi
Brother Convert
Jade
Griffin
Rilla
Reuben
Principal

AUTHOR'S NOTE

The unconventional punctuation is intended
to catch the rhythm of a particular 'street' vernacular.
Although not imperative, it is felt that if this loose
punctuation is adhered to, a greater sense may
be attained from the dialogue.

PRAYER ROOM

Peace be to those who follow righteous guidance

'Truth 'n' Time' by Al Green plays out.

INT. PRAYER ROOM – DAY

An empty prayer room in some college/university.

Paraphernalia from various religions adorn the walls and shelves – books, posters, symbols, statuettes. Behind a door leading into the room, the sound of students passing up and down a squeaky corridor can be heard.

Fiz bustles in, dumps bag, checks time on his watch against the clock on the wall. He has a think.

He dries some residue of water from his hands and round his neck – moving to posters of Christ, Ganesh, Buddha, pulling down little roller-blinds to cover them. Various Hindu, Buddhist and Christian 'idols' are covered with little cloths. He checks the time again. Some girl walks into the room – bag slung over her shoulder, books in hand.

FIZ

D'you fuckin' mind?

The girl exits sharply. Fiz shakes his head, checks his watch one last time, electing that he can't wait any longer. He reaches into his bag and retrieves a prayer-hat, placing it carefully on his head. Next he fetches out a masalla – prayer-mat – flicking it out onto the floor.

Slipping off his shoes, Fiz centres himself and, taking up a standing position at one end of the mat, he begins Salah.

Once Fiz is deep in Salah, the door creaks open and Paul Bunce jitters in – an ex-pillhead, he is continually moving and half-jigging, like there's a perpetual rave going on in his head.

9

Still immersed in prayer, Fiz flicks a look Bunce's way. Bunce 'bunces' around – picking up a book, sitting down, standing up, sniffing – all in the space of a few seconds.

He bunces his way over to where Fiz is assuming the crouch position of the prayer ritual. Bunce just stands bopping and watching Fiz – enthralled. Agitated, Fiz kneels, pressing his forehead to the floor, sits back, forehead on the floor again, then sits back.

BUNCE

You prayin'?

Fiz hasn't finished, closing his eyes and murmuring away.

Oh fuck – sorry. Fuck – sorry. Sorry. Fuckin' 'ell – Jeezus – fuck . . . I'll just, just – I'll wait over 'ere – sorry yeah. (*To himself.*) Sort it out.

Fiz maintains his prayer throughout, whilst Bunce slinks off into a corner – picking up books, but just flicking the pages, furtively.

Fiz promptly finishes prayer, still kneeling on his masalla, but turning to Bunce.

FIZ

I'm gonna put a fuckin' bomb up your arse!

BUNCE

Fuck off – what?! Thought you's finished innit.

FIZ

D'you know how much of a fuckin' sin that is? Fuckin' arsin' about in front of someone when they're doin' Salah?

BUNCE

When you what?

FIZ

When you're prayin'! When you're fuckin' prayin'! S'it fuckin' look like I'm doin'?!

BUNCE

I didn't fuckin' touch you.

FIZ

Don't need to fuckin' touch me – touch me you fuckin' know all about it.

BUNCE

Fuck off.

FIZ

You just don't fuckin' stand there – like a ravin' fuckwit. Got that fuckin' face in my head now innit – (*Mimics Bunce's jig.*) D'you think that fuckin' looks like? I'm tryin' to speak to God, y'get me. I'm like cleansed 'n' washed 'n' pure 'n' shit – I'm like Holy-Ravioli. An' I got this fucked-up fuckin' – (*Mimics again.*) Goin' on in front of me! Jeezus-fuckin'-Christ! What you fuckin' doin' here?

BUNCE
(*trying to calm his jig*)

Ain't fuckin' doin' that.

FIZ

Y'taken your Shahada like?

BUNCE

I ain't takin' nothin' no more.

FIZ

You fuckin' whackhead – ain't a pill. Shahada. La ilaha ilal-lahu Mohammad-ur-rasulullah. 'There is no God but God and Mohammed is his messenger.'

BUNCE
(*beat*)

What about it?

FIZ

You said that? You swore that oath? In a Mosque –
front of witnesses?

BUNCE
(*beat*)

Nah.

FIZ

So if you ain't with the Deen, the fuck you doin' here?
This is Bruvvers Day innit. Ain't no fuckin' junkie-
Jesus shit goin' down here, see what I'm sayin'.

BUNCE

Yeah – s'tomorrow.

FIZ

So back the fuck up and get the fuck out. And take
your – (*Mimics Bunce.*) somewhere fuckin' else.

Bunce doesn't move.

Seriously.

BUNCE
(*mimics Fiz's mimic*)

I don't fuckin' do that alright. Got a fuckin' condition
innit.

FIZ

Fuckin' right.

BUNCE

S'a fuckin' pills.

FIZ

Na-ah!

BUNCE

Not the fuckin' Ecks – the pills they fuckin' got me on
now. S'all the same fuckin' shit at the end of th' day.

FIZ

At the end of the day, you get your fuckin' Kafir arse outta here.

BUNCE

Got some fuckin' Punk innit – said you was lookin' for some, nah?

FIZ

What you got?

BUNCE

Sticky-Punk.

FIZ

Is it.

BUNCE

Yeah Fiz – good shit.

FIZ

S'it propah?

BUNCE

Trus' me yeah – this is some boom-weed, know what I'm sayin'.

FIZ

Much you got?

BUNCE

Gotta bit left.

FIZ

Much – you got it 'ere? You got it now?

BUNCE
(*producing skunk*)

Yeah man – two-five.

FIZ

Nah man – score.

BUNCE

Two-five on the eighth blood.

FIZ

What about half-oz?

BUNCE

Ain't got it.

FIZ

Yeah but how much?

BUNCE

I ain't got it.

FIZ

But what you workin' it at?

BUNCE

I'd do it you for eighty, yeah – but I ain't got it.

FIZ

Eight-O?

BUNCE

Yeah.

FIZ

So that's twenty on the eighth.

BUNCE

Yeah but you're talkin' a half-oz.

FIZ

But you ain't got it.

BUNCE

I can get it you.

FIZ

When?

BUNCE
(*buncing and thinking*)

I can get it . . . coupla hours. Need to gimme the
bread though.

FIZ

I ain't givin' you jack-shit. Gi' you a score for that eighth.

BUNCE

Nah man – two-five.

FIZ

Lemme see the shit.

BUNCE
(*handing over skunk*)
This is some boom-weed bey.

FIZ
(*weighing in hand*)
Bit light, nah?

BUNCE

Nah mate – that's weight. I ain't splicin' nobody outta nuttin'.

FIZ
(*unwrapping skunk*)
Nuff wrappin' bey.

BUNCE

I scaled it up 'fore I wrapped it – shit's gotta be kept moist.

FIZ
(*unwrapping skunk*)
Is it.

BUNCE

Shit's like come over from Amsterdam or some shit.

FIZ

Is it.

Fiz unwraps the skunk a little, squeezing it.

Sticky-shit.

BUNCE

Trus' me yeah.

Fiz lifts skunk to his nose for a whiff.

FIZ
(*sniffing, impressed*)

Yeah Buncy –

BUNCE

Trus' me.

FIZ

Smells like some –

The door snaps open – a couple of Islamic guys enter, one of whom is Brother Kazi.

(*Hiding skunk.*) A'salaam-a-lai-kum.

BROTHER KAZI
(*nodding*)

Wa'la kum salaam.

Brother Kazi and the other Islamic guy just nod back serenely, preparing for prayer.

BUNCE

What d'you say?

FIZ

Let's get outta here a minute – c'mon, move it. (*To Islamic guys.*) Bruvvers, I'll just be a minute, yeah.

BUNCE

'Salami' what?

The Bruvvers nod, as Fiz ushers Bunce out of the door, closing it gently behind them.

INT. PRAYER ROOM – DAY

Rilla sits alone, at a discreet end of the room. A solitary candle burns in a glass jar on the desk in front of her – its flickering flame almost spent. She murmurs some prayers, a prayer book in her hand.

The door bursts open and Bunce bunces into the room.

> BUNCE
> (*to Rilla*)

Alright?

She just nods politely. Bunce holds up his hands – 'I'll leave you to it.'

Rilla goes back to her prayer, whilst Bunce gathers a few scattered chairs, fashioning them into a circle.

Hope it's 'Rapture' today.

She just ignores him – deep in prayer.

The door opens and Matthew Griffin enters in conversation, followed by four other Christians.

> GRIFFIN
> (*entering*)

. . . s'the cause of everything, TV. (*To Bunce.*) Hello Paul.

> BUNCE

Alright – (*Counting bodies.*) Nuff chairs –?

> GRIFFIN

We are but few today – this virus has claimed those of weaker spirit. Glad to see you're here Paul.

> BUNCE

I'm tip-top.

> GRIFFIN

And thank you for the chairs.

BUNCE

Got 'ere early, innit – fuck-all else to do.

GRIFFIN

Paul!

BUNCE

What?

GRIFFIN

This is a House of God /

BUNCE

Oh fuck yeah /

GRIFFIN

Paul!

BUNCE

Sorry sorry sorry – I'm sorry. I'm sorry. (*Hushing his mouth.*) Ssshh-ssshh-sssshhhh.

GRIFFIN

While we occupy this room, this is a House of God – (*Looking to Rilla.*) Even if we have to share it, from time to time – (*Waving.*) Hiya.

Rilla just nods politely.

Won't disturb you. (*To Bunce.*) You should listen very carefully to what I've got to say today – otherwise you will rot in the slime of this earth forever.

Bunce just nods meekly.

(*Sitting.*) Once everyone's settled – (*The group sit.*) I thought today, with all the madness in the world – (*Gesturing to fellow-Christian.*) That we see on every channel, on every box, that we plug into our TVs – it might be that you're thinking – 'Hey, has the Tribulation started or what?' I can assure you it hasn't – otherwise I wouldn't be here talking to you now.

18

The Group chuckle – Bunce a little more exuberantly.

Okay, but getting serious – we all know the clock's ticking towards that single most important event in any Pre-Tribber's life – birth aside – well maybe more actually – as important at least, let's say – yeah, so I thought it might be prudent to ask – how Rapture-Ready do you / feel?

> BUNCE
> (*thumping the air*)

Yes.

> GRIFFIN

Paul –?

> BUNCE

I'm sorry. I'm just like – been waitin' for this. This is it – the Rapture. 'Cause I'm ready. I'm like – (*Shooting to his feet.*) buzzin' with it.

> GRIFFIN

Paul.

> BUNCE
> (*sitting*)

Sorry. Sorry.

> GRIFFIN

You think you're ready?

> BUNCE

Yeah. Yeah. Yeah.

> GRIFFIN

This is life or death – some of us are going to live forever, some of us are going to die. Forever. You think you're going to be one of that lucky number?

> BUNCE
> (*beat*)

I wanna live forever, yeah.

GRIFFIN

Everyone wants to live forever Paul, but not everyone
can – there's not enough room. Heaven isn't some
hotel with beds for all – the Lord chooses who can
stay for eternity, and the rooms are already allocated.
I know I have a reservation – have you done enough
to book your room?

BUNCE

I ain't done nuttin' – sinful.

GRIFFIN

And swearing in God's Own House?

BUNCE

I'm sorry – I said I was sorry. (*Looking to heavens.*)
Sorry.

GRIFFIN

Sometimes Paul, sorry just isn't enough. Words Paul –
that's all they are. The Lord judges us by our actions,
not our words.

BUNCE

Swearin's just words.

GRIFFIN

Yes but, swearing in the House of God.

BUNCE

I can swear outside?

GRIFFIN

No. No. Swearing is the product of an unclean-mind –
full-stop. And the Lord will pass you by if your mind is
not shining with His light.

BUNCE
(*pawing his head*)
How d'you know when it's shinin'?

GRIFFIN

If you don't feel it –?

BUNCE

No I do. I do. I feel somethin' yeah – I'm not sure
what it is.

GRIFFIN

Are you still taking medication?

BUNCE

Yeah, but nah – it ain't that. It's like that space-dust
shi – space-dust stuff – s'only way I can say it. S'like
poppin' in my head – fizzy, know what I mean. (*To
group.*) Sparklin'. You know that stuff? (*The group
murmur.*) Space-dust.

GRIFFIN

When the Rapture comes Paul, you will know. And if
you are not prepared – cleansed of body, mind and
soul /

BUNCE

I am /

GRIFFIN

Paul, you will not go. Look at the clock on that wall –
(*He points.*) This could happen any minute. Choices,
choices, choices – make the right ones, you will be
Raptured. Make the wrong ones – you just bought
a one-way ticket to Post-Trib City. It's that simple.
And you can't say, 'Oh I'll start believing tomorrow.'
Tomorrow is too late. This could happen tonight –
any second – while you're sleeping.

BUNCE

I won't miss it – I'm up all night – the pills /

GRIFFIN

It would not matter if you were wide-awake with your
eyes pinned to the sky. Those who believe /

BUNCE
(*shooting to his feet*)

I do.

GRIFFIN

Sit down Paul!

BUNCE
(*sitting*)
I'm sorry – I got nuff / belief.

GRIFFIN

'For then shall be great Tribulation, such as was not
since the beginning of the world to this time, no, nor
ever shall be' – Matthew twenty-four, twenty-one.
Oh believe it – this is happening. And all these Post-
Tribbers you see laughing now – they'll be screaming –
'I believe, I believe!' (*Flicking look to Rilla.*) But they'll
be too late. The only people to be spared will be the
one hundred and forty-four thousand Jews who see
the error of their ways, by accepting Jesus Christ as
their Lord and Saviour.

BUNCE

Is it. Who they got just now?

Rilla shifts a little, uneasy.

GRIFFIN

Paul, you have no one if you have not accepted Christ
as the Messiah. Not Allah, not Buddha, not Shiva, not
Yaweh – Christ and only Christ. It's only our great
Lord's mercy that will allow these Jews to join us in
Paradise.

RILLA

Excuse me –?

GRIFFIN

Sorry – yes?

                              RILLA
                             (*beat*)
Forget it.

                             GRIFFIN
I'm sorry, is there something –?

                              RILLA
                          (*closing book*)
No. No – it's fine. I'm finished.

With the candle having burnt itself out, she places the jar carefully on a shelf, gathers her things and bustles past the group.

   (*Bustling past.*) Excuse me.

Pausing in the doorway, she draws Griffin and his group a disparaging glance, before exiting with decorum.

                             GRIFFIN
                           (*snorting*)
If that's what it's like sharing with *one* –?!

                             BUNCE
Is there really a hotel?

INT. PRAYER ROOM – DAY

A young woman – Jade – wears a crude Hijab. She sits at a desk, an open book in front of her – nervously chewing gum and reciting. Fiz hovers over her.

                              JADE
                          (*eyes closed*)
La – (*Slight pause.*) La – La-ha-ha –

                               FIZ
                         (*correcting her*)
Ilaha – La ilaha.

                              JADE
Ilaha. (*Referencing book.*) La ilaha ilal /

                               23

FIZ

Don't look at the book. S'the point'a dat? You gotta
know it – (*Fisting his chest.*) By heart. (*Picking up a
Koran.*) There's kids yeah, three years old know d'is
t'ing – whole lot, by heart.

JADE
(*beat*)
I ain't gotta learn all'a dat?

FIZ
You ain't even got the first line down.

JADE
I'm tryin'.

FIZ
S' up? Last night you was rappin' it out quick-time.

JADE
That was in my room though – s'different in here.

FIZ
Ain't nuttin' different – what?

JADE
I don't know, just . . . vibes innit.

FIZ
When we're in here yeah, d'is place is a Mosque, y'get
me – Masjid – 's you call it in Arabic.

JADE
'Mustard'?

FIZ
Don't be silly – not Mustard – Masjid.

JADE
Mas –

FIZ
– jid.

24

                    JADE
Mas-Jid.

                    FIZ
Yeah.

                    JADE
Mmmasjid.

                    FIZ
S'right.

                    JADE
Masjid.

                    FIZ
Alright.

                    JADE
Masjid.

                    FIZ
Alright cool, you got it, yeah. (*Pointing to her book.*)
Now do the same wi' d'is.

                    JADE
Alright. (*Beat.*) Masjid.

                    FIZ
Nah not that.

                    JADE
I know – just, warmin' up innit.

                    FIZ
S'just one line – s'all you gotta learn.

                    JADE
I know.

                    FIZ
So –?

JADE

Alriiight. Pressure. (*Centring herself.*) La – (*Beat.*) Ilaha.

FIZ

S'right –

JADE

Ssshhh. (*Beat.*) I know this – s'Mohammed innit?
Somethin' to do with him.

FIZ
(*exasperated*)
Mohammed-ur-rasu / lullah.

JADE

That's it – what d'I say? / Mohammed –

FIZ

Didn't even make it halfway.

JADE
(*referencing book*)
What is it –?

FIZ
(*beat*)
This ain't good babes.

JADE

What ain't good? I'll get it – I had it last night.

FIZ

In your room. You gotta do this front of an Imam –
in a Mosque.

JADE
(*correcting him*)
Masjid.

FIZ

Don't fuck about.

26

JADE

I ain't fuckin' about.

FIZ

An' don't be cussin' front of no Holy Book.

JADE

Well don't you.

FIZ

Ain't front of me – but I won't. Set an example 'n'
shit. But you gotta listen to me, know what I'm sayin'.

JADE

I am listenin'.

FIZ

F'I'm droppin' some knowledge, you can't be zonin'
out.

JADE
(beat)

Huh?

FIZ

Shit girl – dis what I'm talkin / about.

JADE
(laughing)

I'm joking.

FIZ

You don't know d'is shit, you ain't gonna take Shahada.
You don't take Shahada, you ain't a Muslim. You ain't a
Muslim, I ain't marryin' you. That ain't no joke.

JADE
(beat)

Christ –

FIZ

An' you can forget about him. An' all that Crucifix-
shit you got – I told you to throw that shit out.

                    JADE
D'you mean?

                    FIZ
I told you to get rid of that shit.

                    JADE
I have.

                    FIZ
Don't lie.

                    JADE
What?

                    FIZ
I ain't playin' no games.

                    JADE
What – where?

                    FIZ
I told you I saw the shit – last night. You's at the toilet.

                    JADE
And –?

                    FIZ
You t'ink I got no logic?

                    JADE
What d'you do?

                    FIZ
You got it stashed up – shoebox in your wardro / be.

                    JADE
You fuckin' cunt.

                    FIZ
Hey – the fuckin' Book!

                    JADE
You snoopin' round my room for?!

FIZ

What you stashin' it up for? Shit's supposed to be long
gone.

JADE

I don't believe that.

FIZ

I don't believe you still got the shit.

JADE

It's my jewellery. It's gold.

FIZ

Box of Idols innit.

JADE

I ain't just gonna throw it out – just bin it down the
chute?

FIZ

Sell the shit, I don't know.

JADE

But it's mine.

FIZ

You can't keep it – not in no house'a mine.

JADE

So what –?

FIZ

I told you.

JADE

I'm not throwin' it out. (*Beat.*) I wouldn't ask you to
throw out nuttin' you'd had since you was a child. F'it's
special to you – might not be to anyone else, but is to you.

FIZ
(*beat*)

I would if it was an Idol.

29

JADE

But they're not. They're presents – my Nan gave me
some, and my Mum. For birthdays 'n' things. (*Beat.*)
The ring – s'the last thing my dad ever gave me. I can't
throw that out. Any of it. I can't. (*Beat.*) They're not
Idols. Honestly.

*Fiz stares long and hard at her a moment, slowly taking her in
his arms.*

FIZ

Babes – (*Holding her.*) Maybe you ain't ready for this.

JADE
(*gently sobbing*)

I am. I wanna do it. I do.

FIZ

Well you gotta know – I ain't forcin' you to do nuttin' –

JADE

I know –

FIZ

This gotta be your choice.

JADE

I know.

FIZ

But I ain't marryin' no one, that ain't no Muslim. (*She
looks in his eyes.*) You gotta know d'at.

Jade just nods, breaking free and taking up the prayer book again.

JADE

La – (*Stifling her sobbing.*) I'll get it – La – ila-ha –
(*Pointing to book.*) Can I look a minute?

FIZ

Take a look – but you gotta know the shit by heart.

JADE

I will. I will. (*Reading from book.*) La-illa-ha ilal-lahu /

FIZ

An' you gotta throw dat shit out. (*Beat.*) All dat Idol-shit.

Beat. Jade just nods – not lifting her head from the prayer book.

INT. PRAYER ROOM – DAY

Rilla sits in the same spot as before – in front of her, a candle flickers in a glass jar. A prayer book hangs limply in her hand, as she stares silently through the glowing flame.

A knock on the door breaks her trance – she looks over. Again comes the knock. The door slowly creaks open.

REUBEN
(*slowly peering in*)
Hel-lo – (*Noticing Rilla.*) Oh hi. Sorry to disturb you – is this –? (*Looking round.*) Yeah – guess it is – (*Entering.*) Prayer-Room.

RILLA

Mmm. (*Checking clock on wall.*) They're usually in about half-past.

REUBEN
(*checking clock on wall*)
Okay – thanks. S'it alright – to wait?

She gestures – 'Take a seat.' Reuben perches himself, nervously scanning the room. Rilla resumes her prayer.

Reuben watches her in silence a few moments.

(*Rising to leave.*) Should I wait outside?

RILLA
(*checking clock again*)
They'll be in any minute.

REUBEN

I just feel a little –

RILLA

You're entitled to be here.

REUBEN

But if you're doing Kaddish –

RILLA

Sorry –?

REUBEN

S'no problem, honestly. (*Moving to door.*) I'll wait
outside for the rest.

RILLA

Are you Jewish?

REUBEN
(*grimacing*)

Well yeah – just about.

RILLA

Oh right, no I'm sorry – I thought you were one of the
Christian-Mob.

REUBEN

Christian?! No.

RILLA

Sorry.

REUBEN

I'm pretty severely lapsed, but –

RILLA

No, see – there's a Bible group shares the room.

REUBEN

Oh.

RILLA

That's who I meant – (*Points to clock.*) Half-past.
I thought you were –

REUBEN

Oh, right right, no no. I mean I ain't about to sprout
ringlets, but I put Jewish in my passport.

RILLA

Oh right, well sorry, no – you don't want anything to
do with this lot.

REUBEN

I don't think so. But these guys're comin' in, what –
now?

RILLA
(*looking at clock*)

Any minute – yup.

REUBEN

And the Jewish Society – is that –

RILLA

We share I'm afraid.

REUBEN

An' that's what you're here for?

RILLA

Yeah.

REUBEN

So what normally goes on?

RILLA

Well, the Christians rant a lot – mainly about how all
Jews are going to the Hell-Fire because we don't
believe in their stupid Man-God –

REUBEN

They don't say that.

RILLA

You'll hear for yourself.

REUBEN

No way. So it's like debating and stuff?

RILLA

No they do all the talking.

REUBEN

What – you can't get a word in?

RILLA

No, it's their discussion group. It's their time. They don't really want us here.

REUBEN

I don't understand.

RILLA

By right, we should have a day in here to ourselves – s'way this place is supposed to work – the Christians and the Muslims have got a day and a half each.

REUBEN

And we've got to share?

RILLA

Alright I can understand their argument to a point – but I'm like, 'Hey, multi-faith prayer-room – think maybe we can have some peace and space to ourselves?' (*Gesturing.*) To do Kaddish or whatever –? And they're like – 'Sure, here, have a half-day with these lunatic Christian-Freaks.'

REUBEN

That's out of order. And the Muslims have got, what –?

RILLA

A day and a half.

REUBEN

To themselves? (*She nods.*) No sharing?

RILLA

Nope.

REUBEN

An' the Jewish Society – meets today, an' that's it?

RILLA

S'all they'll give us.

REUBEN

Doesn't seem right.

RILLA

I know.

REUBEN

I mean – is this the twenty-first century?

RILLA

I know.

REUBEN

How come nobody's said anything?

RILLA

I've tried.

REUBEN

I just don't – (*Pointing to her candle.*) Sorry, am I –?

RILLA

No. It's fine.

REUBEN
(*beat*)

Who eh –?

RILLA

My Dad.

35

REUBEN

I'm sorry.

RILLA

S'okay.

REUBEN

Recently, or –?

RILLA

Coming up on five months now.

REUBEN
(*offering hand*)
I'm sorry – Reuben.

RILLA
(*shaking hands*)
Rilla.

REUBEN

Rilla. You're Orthodox or –?

RILLA

Yeah – well no – well my Dad was.

REUBEN

Yeah, same here.

RILLA

Is he –?

REUBEN

No, he's eh . . . he's still alive.

RILLA

That's good.

REUBEN

Mmm.

RILLA
(*beat*)
Well it's good to have you here.

REUBEN

Yeah, well, thanks. I can't believe that – well, a Jewish Society with a Bible-Group?

RILLA

I know. You can't hear yourself think.

REUBEN

And the Bible-Group's gotta another day to itself?

RILLA

No, a day and half. They used to have two full days to themselves – but they were good enough to share a half-day with us.

REUBEN

That's outrageous. How can they get away with that?

RILLA

Oh the same old same old – there's not enough of us to justify giving us a day to ourselves.

REUBEN

Why – how many is there?

The door swings open and Bunce bunces into the room.

BUNCE

Alright.

REUBEN

Hey – hi.

RILLA
(*whispering*)

He's one of them.

REUBEN

What?

BUNCE

Sorry –?

37

RILLA
(*gesturing to Reuben*)
I was talking to him.

BUNCE
Right.

REUBEN
(*whispering*)
Who is he?

BUNCE
(*gathering chairs*)
You want me to put one out for you?

REUBEN
Eh –

RILLA
(*whispering*)
A Jesus-Freak.

REUBEN
Right.

BUNCE
(*holding up chair*)
Yeah –?

REUBEN
Em, sorry – no. No I'm alright.

BUNCE
Ain't a problem.

REUBEN
No I'm /

RILLA
He's here with /

Griffin breezes in with a young woman.

GRIFFIN
(*breezing in*)
We'll need an extra chair today Paul – (*Noticing
Reuben.*) Oh – hi.

REUBEN
Hi.

GRIFFIN
Here for the Scripture-Goup?

RILLA
No.

REUBEN
No – the Jewish Society.

GRIFFIN
Ooommm – two of you now is there?

REUBEN
Two? What?

RILLA
Mmmm, yeah, I was eh –

REUBEN
(*to Rilla*)
What – we're it?

GRIFFIN
Are you actually Jewish?

RILLA
Of course he / is.

REUBEN
Sorry –?

GRIFFIN
We could put a chair out for you.

BUNCE
I aksed him.

39

                    REUBEN
No, I'm Jewish.

                    GRIFFIN
                    (*beat*)
Are you sure?

                    RILLA
What –?!

                    REUBEN
Mate, I'll tell you, right now – I'm surer than I've ever
been.

                    GRIFFIN
                    (*beat*)
Well we've always been a discussion Group – you do
know that?

                    RILLA
Yeah right.

                    GRIFFIN
Excuse me –?

                    REUBEN
Alright, just – take it easy, okay? Things've changed,
but, we'll work something out.

                    GRIFFIN
Oh nothing's changed as far as we're concerned. This
time has always been block-booked as Scripture-
Group discussion – it's on the board.

                    REUBEN
Okay.

                    GRIFFIN
Go and look.

                    RILLA
We know.

GRIFFIN

We have our discussion – you sit in the corner with
your candle.

REUBEN

Hey!

RILLA

You fucking prick.

BUNCE

Oi! Sort it out.

GRIFFIN

How you can use that language in here. Well I'll tell you
– if anything's changed, it's your situation, not ours.

REUBEN

Okay – just chill out.

GRIFFIN

I am in the House of God – I am perfectly 'chilled'
thank you.

RILLA

You are such a hypocrite.

GRIFFIN

Me –?! 'Woe unto you, scribes and Pharisees,
hypocrites! For ye shut up the kingdom of heaven
against men.' / Matthew twenty-three, thirteen.

REUBEN

Hey, alright, / alright.

RILLA

What'd I tell you?

BUNCE

Everyone just chill it down a few b.p.m.'s.

GRIFFIN

Paul, it's okay. They are welcome to stay, as long as

they respect our right to use the room for discussion –
as we shall respect their right to remain, in silent
prayer.

REUBEN

You can't say that.

RILLA

That's nothing. That's mild.

GRIFFIN

That was the deal.

RILLA

Deal –?!

REUBEN

Well who made that? It's gotta change. Who do we
speak to?

GRIFFIN
(*barbed point to Rilla*)
Oh – she knows fine.

Reuben turns to Rilla – she looks a little evasive.

INT. PRAYER ROOM – DAY

*A small group of Muslims, including Fiz, Jade, Brother Kazi
and Sister Malik, sit listening attentively as Brother Convert
takes the floor.*

BROTHER CONVERT

Peace be to those who follow righteous guidance.
(*Beat.*) Not long after I took my Shahada –
Alhamdulillah – a friend of mine – a good friend that
I'd known since way back – she came to me and said,
'Religion is nothing but a security blanket. How can
there be a God, with so much suffering in the world?'
She was an old friend, entitled to her opinion, and
I have to say, I didn't have an answer at the time. But

the gist of what she said – in putting my Faith, my Life, my Death, in some, unseen God's hands, I was making a fool of myself – that stayed with me. I have to say it never put any doubts into my mind – I just wondered about her mind. For me, I guess it sounded kinda ungrateful. She was an old friend. (*Beat.*) Then coupla years ago, somethin' happened that made me think about what she said. I don't know if you guys remember the stories – it was back in the States – these doctors were being sued because they had broken a rib or two when giving heart massage on a dying patient? You know how sick that made me feel – I thought the ungrateful sh – (*Beat.*) Now in Islam, ungrateful is what Kafir means – those who deny. So if someone is ungrateful to a doctor who injures them in saving their life – what about the creator of that heart and the whole body, who could start and stop it when He chooses? Who created you, me, my friend, the doctors being sued, the patients, everyone and everything – what would you think of someone who was ungrateful to God? Is God not more worthy of our praise and our love than a mere doctor who could help us get better, or restore our sight or health – but only really if God allows him to do so? When you realise this, you realise to deny God like your friends or family might do – or to associate a partner to God like most Christians do, in Jesus – is the ultimate sin, as it is being ungrateful to our shared Creator, who could take it all away in an instant and yet neither do we take time to thank Him or deny Him entirely. How ungrateful is this? The whole point of yours and my existence is to see if we will acknowledge the Creator or not, and worship him how he wants us to. To do otherwise, is to be ungrateful to God. (*Beat.*) As for all the suffering in the world – sure, Man might say he's doing it in the name of God – but God's not pulling the trigger. (*Beat.*) Thank you.

43

Brother Convert takes a seat to some polite applause – Fiz
applauding a little more raucously. Brother Kazi gets to his feet.

> BROTHER KAZI
> (*applauding*)
> Ma'shallah Bruvver, Ma'shallah. I think we can all
> safely say, we wish there was more Americans like you
> – innit.

The small group applaud again.

> (*Applauding.*) Innit. In every way. (*Applause dies down.*)
> And you can see more of the Bruvver's story about his
> conversion to Islam on – (*To Brother Convert.*) It's
> DVD right?

> BROTHER CONVERT
> Y'know, I didn't bring them.

> BROTHER KAZI
> You ain't got 'em?

> BROTHER CONVERT
> No – I forgot to bring them.

> BROTHER KAZI
> But it's DVD – right?

> BROTHER CONVERT
> Yes, there is a DVD – (*To Group.*) I'm sorry, I just
> completely – but check out the website.

> BROTHER KAZI
> That's right, there's a website – Sistah Malik's got
> some flyers – (*To Sister Malik.*) You got 'em – right?
> (*She nods, flyers aloft.*) But just before you go Bruvvers
> and Sistahs – got quite an important announcement to
> make, yeah. Keep in your mind alright, that this is just
> some temporary thing – but you won't be able to use
> the room for prayer this Friday.

The Group murmur, disgruntled.

44

FIZ

What?! S'goin' down?

BROTHER KAZI

Listen yeah, listen – I spoke to the Principal this
morning yeah, I told him – don't matter what day we
lose, no way we're losin' Friday.

FIZ

Y'talkin' about – shouldn't be losin' nuttin'.

BROTHER KAZI

Bruvvers and Sistahs, you know these is difficult times
to be a Muslim in this country, so I want you all to be
patient and we'll sort this problem out. S'just a mix
up. I don't want no radical-action.

JADE
(*to Fiz*)

What is the problem –?

FIZ

I don't know – (*To Brother Kazi.*) Yeah Bruvver Kazi –
what is the problem?

BROTHER KAZI

They've had to move things about this week – we'll
sort it out – but the Jews is aksin' for their own day, so
they gonna give 'em it.

The Group murmur.

FIZ

So they takin' it off us?

BROTHER KAZI

Nobody's takin' nuttin' off nobody – alright. They
gotta move things round, it's a temporary thing, we're
gonna sit down, sort it out, an' we ain't gonna lose
nuttin'. Definitely not Friday.

45

FIZ

Not nuttin'.

BROTHER KAZI

It's this Friday and that's all. We'll see if we can make
some temporary provisions – alright? (*Turning to
Brother Convert.*) So I just wanna thank our American
Bruvver for comin' in – (*Group applaud again.*) And if
I'm not in any of your classes, I'll see you on Friday
for Jumma – but not here. As-salaam a lai kum.

*The Group murmur back a disgruntled 'Salaam', gather their
things and exit – Sister Malik handing out flyers at the door,
before following on behind Brother Kazi and Brother Convert.*

*Fiz remains behind with Jade – who is still wearing her crude
hijab badly.*

JADE

Sal – Salaam a – Slaam a – laykoom. Slam-a-laykoom.
I'm alright with that – long 's I say it slowly. Slam-
a-laykoom. Yeah, I quite like it actually. S'it mean
again?

FIZ

You believe that shit –?

JADE

Slam-a-laykoom. Yeah what's it mean?

FIZ

Eh?

JADE

S'it mean?

FIZ

What?

JADE

Slam-a-laykoom.

46

FIZ

What?

JADE

S'it mean?

FIZ

Oh right. Eh – 'Peace and Blessings upon you.'

JADE

Really?

FIZ

Yeah.

JADE

That's really – slam-a-laykoom – peace and – wa' is
it –?

FIZ

Blessings upon you.

JADE

'Peace and blessings upon you.' That's really nice.
Slam-a-laykoom.

FIZ

Yeah, yeah, alright.

JADE

Who made that up?

FIZ

God.

JADE

Is it. That's amazing.

FIZ

He ain't gonna sort out jack-shit.

JADE

What – who?

FIZ

Bruvver Kazi. I mean, he's alright – but he don't know how to handle these folk.

JADE

Who's he handlin'?

FIZ

These fuckin' Jews. And the fuckin' Christians – fuckin' Kafirs. You heard the guy didn't ya –?

JADE

What – the American geezer –?

FIZ

Yeah. You heard what he said – fuckin' Kafirs're ungrateful innit. Can't trust 'em. (*Beat.*) They ain't gettin' us outta here.

JADE
(*beat*)

You used to call me a Kafir.

FIZ

Yeah but babes – technically you was. But you on the right path now innit. You take your Shahada, that's it – you pure like a baby – guaranteed Paradise, y'get me. 'Long as you don't sin no more.

JADE
(*beat*)

I can have a puff.

FIZ

Nah, not after / Shahada.

JADE

No way – 'bout you?!

FIZ

Nah.

JADE

D'you mean 'Nah'? You're skinnin' up every two
minutes.

FIZ

S'different.

JADE

Oh right, here it comes.

FIZ

Seriously listen to me – I's born a Muslim innit.

JADE

So –?

FIZ

So any sins yeah – like bad habits 'n' shit – f'I picked
that shit up before I totally understood how it all
works 'n' shit – ain't my fault.

JADE

Ah no way!

FIZ

Seriously listen – I'm tellin' you how the shit works, so
when you take your Shahada, and become a Muslim,
you already know everythin', so you ain't got no excuse.

JADE
(*beat*)

Seriously?

FIZ

Tellin' ya.

JADE
(*beat*)

So don't fuckin' tell me any more.

FIZ

I gotta – s'for your own good.

JADE

Fuckin' good is it if I can't have a puff?

FIZ

Hey – s'a Masjid remember.

JADE

Soddin' hell then – can I say that?

FIZ

Still cussin'.

JADE

Can I do anythin'?

FIZ

Look – you're gonna be pure, alright?

JADE

I don't wanna be pure.

FIZ

Yeah you do.

JADE

But it's me that's doin' everythin'.

FIZ

Y'talkin' about?

JADE

Well I am. I ain't seein' none of my old crew no more /
and

FIZ

Y'better not be. They ain't nuttin' but Shay'tans – you
know that – every one of them. Gettin' you into bad
shit – that what you wanna do –?

JADE

No.

FIZ

You wanna go back to that shit?

JADE

No – tch. But if I ain't drinkin' – gotta have a puff at least.

The door opens and some Dungeons and Dragons Geeks begin to enter, carrying game boards under their arms.

FIZ
(*to geeks*)
Two fuckin' minutes alright.

The Geeks about-turn, closing the door behind them.

Listen yeah – there's some serious shit goin' down here.

JADE

I know.

FIZ

Yeah –?

JADE
Too right – if you're puffin' I'm puffin'.

FIZ
Not that! Fuckin' 'ell – do what you fuckin' want.

JADE

I will.

FIZ
The room. These fuckin' Kafirs. They think we're stupid, but I got their moves.

JADE
Yeah what was that about Friday?

FIZ
S'at I'm sayin' – they think they can sneak us outta here – stop us prayin' – move us some place, way out wherever, an' tell us it's just some temporary shit.

JADE

S'at what they're doin'?

FIZ

S'at they think they gonna do.

JADE

Fuckin' Kafirs.

FIZ

Yeah – well I ain't prayin' in no refugee-camp.

INT. PRAYER ROOM – DAY

The room is in blackout. Sound of keys turning in lock – the door opens, light spilling in from the main thoroughfare. Rilla stands silhouetted in the doorway, staring into the darkened room a moment – she flicks on the lights.

As the bulbs pop into life, Rilla enters, closing door behind her and giving the keys a little squeeze before hanging them on a nearby designated hook.

She enjoys being alone in the room a second – before crossing to her glass jar, resting on its shelf. She moves with the jar to her usual corner spot, producing a candle from her bag, placing it inside the jar. She lights the wick, staring at the flame as it takes hold – then surveys the big empty room.

She thinks a moment, before lifting the jar, and relocating to a desk in the centre of the room. Placing the jar on its new perch, she gazes round the room again. A mobile phone rings. She looks up at the clock on the wall, crossing the room to fetch her bag.

She retrieves the ringing phone from her bag, staring at the caller-ID, unsure whether or not to answer.

A knock on the door and Reuben enters – a bag slung over his shoulder. Rilla's phone rings off.

REUBEN
(*entering*)
Hel-lo – this Scripture-Group?

RILLA
Not any more – thank Christ. Good to see you.

REUBEN
Yeah – you too. (*Pointing to candle.*) Sorry, you –?

RILLA
No. I mean I will, but – not quite the same mad rush now.

REUBEN
I know – when I got your text I thought – 'Sheee, that girl ain't messin' about.' The hell d'you say to him?

RILLA
The Principal?

REUBEN
Yeah – I said I'd come with you.

RILLA
No I think /

REUBEN
Not that you needed me – sorry.

RILLA
No I think the email you sent really helped.

REUBEN
Yeah? Was that, was that alright?

RILLA
No, that was really good.

REUBEN
Yeah? 'Cause I just put in what we talked about – well you saw it.

RILLA

Yeah.

REUBEN

I mean I didn't want to lay it on too thick –

RILLA

No, it was fine.

REUBEN

Come across as some mad Zealot – but if you reckon
it helped –?

RILLA

No it did.

REUBEN

So that's it, it's official – this is our day?

RILLA

Half-day.

REUBEN

Yeah but – it's ours – we got it. Well you did.

RILLA

Needed both of us – but yeah.

REUBEN

Well yeah, but – that's amazin' – (*Offering his hand.*)
Mazel-Tovs all round.

RILLA

Mazel-Ttov.

*Their handshake becomes a stolen embrace – Rilla's ringing
mobile quickly breaking them up. She checks the caller-ID.*

REUBEN

I don't mind if you wanna –?

RILLA
(*rejecting call*)
No – (*Ringing stops.*) S'nothing.

Reuben hoists his bag up onto the desk.

REUBEN

Got somethin' for you – well us – the room.

RILLA

(watching him rummage)

What is it –?

REUBEN

(rummaging)

Show you – d'you bring anythin' in?

RILLA

No. What've you got –?

REUBEN

This –

He produces a bottle of wine.

RILLA

Aw – sweet.

REUBEN

(rummaging again)

That's not it. And – this –

Reuben produces a heavy, ornate, half-size silver Torah from his bag, hinged vertically down the middle, engraved with menorahs and decorated with little chain tassels. He places it proudly on the table.

This a propah Shul now or what?

RILLA

Oh my God – *(Steps back.)* What's that?

REUBEN

S'it look like –?

RILLA

A Torah?

REUBEN

Yeah –

He opens the Torah, revealing the scroll inside.

RILLA

You're not going to touch it –?

REUBEN
(*not touching scroll*)
S'alright – don't know if it's the full thing – writing's quite small.

RILLA

But – how come you've got it?

REUBEN

Had it lyin' around for years. Thought I'd donate it to the – well it's for you really – but I thought it'd be good to keep it here.

RILLA
(*taking a look*)
I mean, it's beautiful, but – where d'you get it?

REUBEN

Kinda passed down to me – an old family friend – Joe Klein.

RILLA

Was he a Rabbi?

REUBEN

Nah. He was the Sweet-Man.

RILLA

What – like a Mensch?

REUBEN

Nah, I mean he gave me sweets /

RILLA

Oh.

REUBEN

S'why he was the Sweet-Man. My dad used to take me
round – to his place, his house – and I'd always see
this – just sittin' up there, on the shelf.

RILLA

Mmm.

REUBEN

I used to love goin' round there, it was just like, sweet
heaven. Every time.

RILLA

Kinda like a nice Uncle?

REUBEN

Kinda. He had this sauna –

RILLA

A sauna?

REUBEN

Yeah, in his house /

RILLA

Back then?

REUBEN

It was kinda weird. I thought he was a great guy – well,
he was, to me – but he used to fill his sauna full of
little girls.

RILLA

No?!

REUBEN

Yeah, he'd always be walkin' round in just a – like an
old bath-robe. It was only years later it occurred to
me.

RILLA

That's awful.

REUBEN
I thought he was just like, nice to kids.

RILLA
You didn't go in – the sauna? He didn't make you –?

REUBEN
God no! I don't even want to think about it –
(*Shivers.*) Ai-yi-yi. No. No. Nothing like that. Just
sweets.

RILLA
Mmm.

REUBEN
Yeah, but when he died, I think my dad ended up with
it, then I ended up with it, but – s'yours now.

RILLA
Mmm.

REUBEN
Seriously – you can keep it.

RILLA
Mmm – thanks.

REUBEN
Mean – you can take it home if you want –

RILLA
Em –

REUBEN
But I thought it might be quite nice here.

RILLA
Yeah – probably better here.

REUBEN
Yeah, thought it'd be nice.

RILLA
(*looking at text*)
Can you read Hebrew?

REUBEN
At my Barmitzvah – don't think I've said a word since.
You –?

RILLA
I wish – love to learn.

REUBEN
Yeah be good to get it back. Could never understand
a word I was sayin' though.

RILLA
Were you shittin' yourself?

REUBEN
At my Barmitzvah?

RILLA
Yeah.

REUBEN
You not got any Brothers?

RILLA
No – just me.

REUBEN
And you never –?

RILLA
No I never had a Batmitzvah. I wanted to, but –

REUBEN
Nah you didn't. You don't know how lucky you are.
I mean being a Jewish-guy – seriously. Eight days old an'
they cut half your dick off – (*She laughs.*) S'not funny. I
mean I ain't sayin' I remember it – but that's gotta cause
some serious deep, deep psychological torment.

RILLA

Oh c'mon.

REUBEN

What?! Half-mutilate you, then parade you in front of friends and family you probably won't see again 'til, I don't know –

RILLA

Your Barmitzvah –?

REUBEN

Yeah – exactly. Just when you're gettin' over that first major embarrassment, they're like – 'Yeah, let's put him in this massive suit, and get him up on the Bimah for a laugh. And get him to read some Hebrew that means absolutely nothing to him for half an hour.'

RILLA

Oh c'mon – it's good for you.

REUBEN

I dunno – yeah your Dad's full of naches, your mum won't stop cryin', your mates are takin' the piss and everyone else is like – 'Look how much you've grown, what a size – I haven't seen you since your Bris.' Good for them maybe – dunno 'bout me.

RILLA

But you get pressies – no?

REUBEN

They gotta give you somethin' after thirteen years of torture! But yeah, the pressies are good –

Rilla's mobile rings again.

(*Gesturing.*) Sorry – you wanna –?

RILLA

Sorry – (*She checks the caller-ID, again rejecting the call.*) Oh piss off.

REUBEN
(*beat*)

Everythin' okay?

RILLA

Yes, no fine.

REUBEN

Sure –? I don't mind if you wanna –?

RILLA

No it's nothing. Sorry. (*Beat.*) Yeah, what does your
Dad do?

REUBEN

He eh – officially he works the stock market.
Unofficially he's unemployed.

RILLA

Oh. How old is he?

REUBEN

He's what – sixty-four –?

RILLA

Oh, so he's retired?

REUBEN

No. No. He's been unemployed for years.

RILLA

Oh. (*Beat.*) Does your Mum work?

REUBEN

No. My Dad's only got one leg.

RILLA
(*chuckling*)

He hasn't.

REUBEN

No – he has.

RILLA

What – seriously –? (*Reuben is serious.*) Oh – I'm really sorry.

REUBEN

No it's fine – been like that since – 'bout as long as I can remember him.

RILLA

Really?

REUBEN

Yeah.

RILLA

What eh . . . why did he need to –?

REUBEN

I dunno – some kind of cancer that became like, gangrene or somethin'. (*Beat.*) I remember goin' into hospital to see him, just before he eh, had it off – I was eight – an' it was a pretty major operation back then /

RILLA

Well yeah.

REUBEN

I mean it still is.

RILLA

Of course – (*Sizing up her leg.*) Where did he eh – just below the knee –?

REUBEN

Oh no, no – (*Hand on her leg.*) 'Bout there – half-way up his thigh.

RILLA

Ai-yi-yi.

REUBEN

Yeah I remember being at his bedside, and he looked
me right in the eye and said, 'I may not make it
through this, son. S'up to you now to look after your
mother and sister.'

RILLA

He said that?

REUBEN

Yeah – just before the operation.

RILLA

That's serious.

REUBEN

I know. I'm like eight years old and thinkin', 'Shit, I'm
the Head of the Family now.'

RILLA

You just got one sister –?

REUBEN

Yeah – but I'm like preparing myself for this, taking
over from my Dad – I'm eight, but I'm like seriously
psyching myself up for this. An' then my Mum
comes out and says, 'S'okay – your dad's gonna be
fine.'

RILLA

That must've been some feeling.

REUBEN

Yeah. (*Beat.*) I was really upset.

RILLA

'Upset?' But he was okay – no?

REUBEN

Well – he was alive, but . . . the day we picked him up –
the way he kinda just, hobbled out to meet us – this
walk. This pathetic – (*Slight pause.*) I just thought,

'Why did you tell me? I was ready to be Head of the House,' I mean, I was ready. I'd worked my mind into this place and 'Now what am I suppose to do? Accept this, Half-Man back as Head?'

RILLA

You were only eight.

REUBEN

I know – took me another ten years to get outta there.

RILLA
(*beat*)

Suppose it's honest.

REUBEN

He should never've done that.

RILLA

Yeah but – you can understand where he's coming from?

REUBEN

Yeah but – he was the adult, I was the kid. He shoulda known that you can't go sayin' that to an eight-year-old, 'less you mean it.

RILLA

You'd rather he died?

REUBEN

No. Well I don't know. (*Beat.*) All I know is things ain't been right between us since.

RILLA
(*resonating with him*)

Yeah –?

Rilla's mobile rings yet again.

REUBEN

I think maybe someone's tryin' to get a hold of you.

She once more lifts the phone – checking the caller-ID.

> RILLA
> (*rejecting call*)

Mmm.

> REUBEN
> (*beat*)

Same person?

> RILLA

Mmm. (*Turning off phone.*) I'll turn it off – I'm really sorry. (*Beat.*) S'off.

> REUBEN
> (*beat*)

Who is it?

> RILLA

Oh it's –

> REUBEN
> (*beat*)

It's nothin' urgent, or –?

> RILLA

No. No. I've turned it off now, so –

> REUBEN

Sure there's nothin' –?

> RILLA
> (*beat*)

It's my Mum.

> REUBEN

Ah. You don't wanna speak t' her?

> RILLA

Not particularly, no. (*Beat.*) She knew about the hoo-ha with the room – think she just wants to say 'Mazel-Tov'.

REUBEN

Oh right – I don't mind. Give her a call – I'm good
with Mums.

RILLA

No I don't want to speak to her – if you don't mind –?

REUBEN

No, no problem – s'your Mum.

RILLA

Mmm. She is.

REUBEN
(*beat*)

Must be hard for you's.

RILLA

She's hiding it well.

REUBEN

Mmm. (*Beat.*) S'just the two of you though – right?

RILLA

Unfortunately. (*Beat.*) She's so full of shit.

REUBEN

Why what's she / ?

RILLA

Well trying to phone up and be all – 'Oh your father
would be so proud' – she doesn't give a shit about him.

REUBEN

I'm sure she does.

RILLA

Oh no – I'm sure she doesn't.

REUBEN

Have you spoken to her, or –?

RILLA

There's no point.

REUBEN

I dunno – maybe you's should sit down an' –

RILLA

Oh, we've talked – screamed, cried, begged – done all of that. I've given up.

REUBEN

You said it's been, what – five months or so –?

RILLA

Exactly!

REUBEN

What?

RILLA

She can't even wait.

REUBEN

'Wait'?

RILLA

She couldn't even wait two months, never mind eleven.

REUBEN

Why what she do?

RILLA

She's made a complete fool of my Dad – and everything he ever was or stood for. Our family, everything – it was all just a lie for her. We were all just living a lie. She never cared about him, or me – every word, every minute, every meal, every birthday, every second of every single day – nothing but a lie. 'It's not something I planned dear . . .' (*Beat.*) Not something she planned. 'You want me to accept you're fucking another Man – not two months after my father – your husband – That picture beside your bed ring any bells? Not two months after we put his body in the ground, you want me to say, "Oh Mum, go with your heart, 'cause Dad wouldn't want you to be alone" – you want me to say that?'

67

REUBEN

Shit.

RILLA

Well I won't. I won't. (*Beat.*) I've got to show my face in this place every day.

REUBEN

What does anyone here know?

RILLA

And she's prancing about the place like some fucking bitch in heat! How can that woman be my Mother?! Oh an' you know the best bit? She said, 'In time, if you want to call him Dad, I'm sure he won't mind.' 'He won't mind?' 'Oh well that's alright then – long as he's happy and you're happy, then I suppose me and Dad – my real Dad, my biological dad – who's decomposing as we speak – then yeah, yeah – we're really happy for you too.'

REUBEN
(*beat*)
I gotta say – does seem a bit quick.

RILLA

A bit?!

REUBEN

I mean, don't know how I'd feel about – losin' my Dad. But havin' to call some other guy 'Dad' –?

RILLA

Well he can rot before I ever say it. They both can.

REUBEN

Is he Jewish?

She shakes her head.

No?!

RILLA

No. He's nothing. (*Beat.*) She knew exactly what she was doing.

REUBEN

I'm really sorry.

RILLA
(*containing tears*)
It's just my Dad – I miss him so much. So much.

Reuben reaches out, taking Rilla in his arms – her tear-banks about to burst.

REUBEN
(*comforting her*)
Ah come here. S'okay – ssshh.

RILLA
(*fighting tears*)
He doesn't deserve this –

REUBEN
Ssshh, ssshh – s'okay – I know.

RILLA
I'm trying – but that woman – I just wanna /

The door crashes open and Fiz enters brusquely with Jade – he's carrying a masalla, she's wearing her hijab and nonchalantly chewing gum.

Reuben breaks from Rilla – stepping forward.

REUBEN
(*to Fiz*)

Hey –?!

Jade perches herself on a desk – eyeballing Reuben and Rilla. Fiz ignores Reuben and Rilla, clearing a few chairs aside to make a space.

Excuse me – hey, I'm talkin' to you –? What d'you
think you're doin'?

*Fiz point-blank refuses to acknowledge Reuben. Space cleared, he
flicks his masalla out on the floor.*

Excuse me – can you not do that?

*Fiz slips off his shoes and takes up a standing position at one end
of the prayer-mat.*

No, hey – I'm askin' you not to do that. (*To Jade.*) Are
you with him –?

Fiz begins Salah.

(*Approaching Fiz.*) I'm sorry, but you can't /

JADE
Don't fuckin' touch him.

Reuben stops – looking to Jade.

REUBEN
What's your problem –?

Jade just chews – eyeballing Reuben.

No he can't do that – so can you get him outta here –?

Jade just stares and chews. Fiz continues Salah.

(*To Fiz.*) Listen mate I'm sorry – can you please stop
now –?

Fiz continues Salah.

You're showin' me some serious disrespect – I ain't
done nuttin' to you.

Fiz continues Salah.

Mate, we're in the middle of quite a personal
discussion, this is the Jewish Society and alright, you

used to have the room on a Friday, but – you don't
any more, I'm sorry.

Jade chews gum. Fiz continues Salah.

Look, you're bein' totally out of order. I mean what's
wrong with you? Go – don't you get it?

Fiz continues Salah.

Seriously – can you please leave?

Fiz continues Salah.

If you're tryin' to make some pathetic point – okay,
yeah, great, wow, well done, News at Ten – but can
you go now please?

Fiz prays. Jade chews.

RILLA

Get fucking out!

REUBEN

Rilla – s'alright. (*To Fiz.*) Mate really, honestly, this is
gettin' really fuckin' stupid now, so can you just stop
wherever you're at and get the fuck outta here – I'm
not askin', I'm tellin'.

Fiz continues Salah.

Mate, I don't know what your problem is, but you're
takin' the fuckin' piss now – I will throw you out.

Fiz continues Salah.

You ain't stayin' –

Fiz maintains Salah, as Reuben moves in.

JADE

Touch him you die!

Reuben refrains a moment.

REUBEN
(*to Jade*)
Listen you can sit there mouthin' off all you fuckin'
want – makes no difference to me. He's moving – you
can take him, he can do it, or I'll do it.

Jade eyeballs Reuben, confidently chewing.

RILLA
She's not even a Muslim.

Jade looks Rilla's way.

Are you? (*Jade remains silent.*) I mean she might tell
him that – (*Gestures to Fiz.*) But he's never gonna
know what she really feels – (*To Jade.*) Is he?

Jade chews a little slower. Fiz squirms in his prayer.

(*To Reuben.*) How can he look in her heart? (*To Jade.*)
I mean yeah, you can say you are – you can wear the
scarf and fetch his sticks when he throws them – but
you can always stay the same inside.

REUBEN
(*to Jade*)
You're not a Muslim?

Jade chews ever slower.

RILLA
She's obviously not got a choice – (*To Jade.*) S'that
what's happening – d'you need someone to talk to –?

Jade remains silent.

Just wink if you need help –

Jade remains silent.

Okay – we'll talk later.

Fiz flicks a look up to Jade from his prayer.

JADE

What – I didn't say nuttin'.

RILLA

Ssshh – s'okay.

JADE
(*stepping forward*)
Fuck you – I didn't say nuttin' to you bitch.

REUBEN

Alright that's it.

JADE

What'd I say to you – I didn't say nuttin'. She's a lyin'
Jew-bitch /

REUBEN

Watch your fuckin' / mouth!

JADE
(*moving to Rilla*)
I'll stab your fuckin' eyes out bitch.

REUBEN

Look just get the fuck outta here alright.

Rilla ducks for cover, while Reuben moves to grab Jade.

FIZ
(*kneeling on masalla*)
Touch her an' I'll kill ya.

REUBEN

Mate you're full of shit. I ain't fuckin' listenin' to you
an' I ain't fuckin' scared. That what this is about – we
supposed to be?

FIZ

Touch her yeah – I'll kill ya.

REUBEN

Yeah, right, sure, whatever – 'Death to Jews' – just get the fuck out.

JADE
(*to Fiz*)

I didn't say nuttin' – she's a lyin' fuckin' bitch.

REUBEN
(*to Jade*)

Why don't you shut the fuck up?

JADE
(*to Rilla*)

In't ya? Bitch? Yeah you – hello – yeah you bitch – what you sayin' now – huh?

REUBEN
(*to Fiz*)

I'm not askin' you / again.

JADE
(*to Rilla*)

I'm talkin' to you / bitch.

REUBEN
(*to Fiz*)

Get her the fuck outta / here.

JADE
(*to Rilla*)

What you sayin' now?! 'Cause you're talkin' shit in't ya? Lyin' / fuckin' bitch.

REUBEN
(*to Jade*)

Hey don't go fuckin' near / her.

JADE

You're talkin' fuckin' shit – I didn't say nuttin' / to you.

REUBEN

What's wrong with you's?!

JADE

I didn't say nuttin' so don't fuckin' / lie, alright.

REUBEN

Just get the fuck out!

RILLA
(*to Jade*)

I'm not livin' the lie.

JADE

What?!

REUBEN

Rilla –

JADE
(*going after Rilla*)

Come here you fuckin' bitch!

REUBEN
(*going after Jade*)

Oi – leave her / alone.

JADE

Gonna fuckin' kill ya.

Scrambling to get at Rilla, Jade sends the open Torah crashing to the ground – the scroll flailing across the floor.

REUBEN

Not the Torah!

JADE
(*to Rilla*)

You're fuckin' / dead.

RILLA

That's our Torah – you fucking animal!

Rilla and Jade go at each other.

> **REUBEN**
> Rilla – fuckin' hell! Get off her you fuckin' slag!

Reuben leaps across to intervene.

> **FIZ**
> (*rising from masalla*)
> Fuckin' Kafir – I told you don't touch her.

Rilla thumps the emergency alarm as Fiz piles into the action, grappling with Reuben – the Torah scrolls are ripped in the mayhem.

> **REUBEN**
> (*grappling with Fiz*)
> You fuckin' prick! Get out!

> **FIZ**
> (*grappling with Reuben*)
> Gonna fuckin' kill ya – Kafiiir! I'll fuckin' kill ya!
> Thievin' fuckin' Kafir!

Students pile into the room to break up the fight and drag everyone out – except Rilla.

With the sound of the bell still ringing and the riot fading off down the corridor, Rilla makes her way to the shredded scrolls. She gathers them together, planting gentle kisses on the ragged Torah, as the lights fade.

INT. PRAYER ROOM – DAY

In blackout, a solitary voice is heard.

> **GRIFFIN**
> (*voice-over, in blackout*)
> 'Enter ye in at the strait gate – for wide is the gate, and
> broad is the way, that leadeth to destruction, and
> many there be which go in thereat. Because strait is

the gate, and narrow is the way, which leadeth unto life, and few there be that find it.'

Lights fade up on the Bible-Group – Griffin at the helm, Bunce amongst the several gathered Christians.

Matthew, chapter seven – verses thirteen and fourteen. (*Beat.*) Wide indeed is the Gate that leads to destruction. And I'm sure we're all aware that last week, in this room – that gate was open and some people chose to walk right through it – people who claim to believe in God. But the Lord we know – the one true God – has made it clear to us, that we are the few – out of the billions and billions of people who ever lived – that will be able to find the Strait Gate.

BUNCE
But it's the narrow one innit.

GRIFFIN
Paul –?

BUNCE
S'like a test innit. 'Cause everyone's gonna be like – 'Look at that gate, it's like well wide – s'gotta be the way in – innit.' But it ain't.

GRIFFIN
Very good Paul.

BUNCE
S'like a trap – innit.

GRIFFIN
A test.

BUNCE
Yeah but it's a trap – 'cause once you walk through yeah – the eh, Gates a' Destruction – they ain't gonna let you out – is it. No way. (*To Group.*) S'a trap.

GRIFFIN

A trap, yes – for the 'many'. But the 'few' shall find the narrow-gate.

BUNCE

Yeah but listen – you're gonna have to scope 'em both out, innit – s'what I been thinkin'.

GRIFFIN

What –?

BUNCE

Well you ain't just gonna walk through the first gate you see – is it. (*To Group.*) Is it. You're gonna have to check 'em both out. Mean how narrow we talkin' – garden gate, Lord a' the Rings ting, or what? You ain't gonna know, 'less you check it out.

GRIFFIN

Paul – the Lord will guide the 'Few'.

BUNCE

Yeah? Well I reckon we should check 'em both out – gotta be sure innit. S'a test.

GRIFFIN

You do that Paul. But the point I was trying to make – if other Groups are tempted towards this path – destruction – we should not follow. What we can do, is what we have been doing, and set an example to these people, so they might accept Our Lord Jesus Christ as their saviour – and maybe find the narrow gate for themselves. (*Beat.*) Now the college Principal /

BUNCE

What if they follow us?

GRIFFIN

What – who?

78

BUNCE

There's gonna be 'nuff folk – billions innit – looking
for, what – two gates? They see us sneakin' off, then –
I dunno –

GRIFFIN

One minute Paul – okay?

BUNCE

Yeah, yeah, sorry. Just – f'your name's not down,
shouldn't be gettin' in – gotta be careful, know what
I'm sayin'.

GRIFFIN

Well don't be so sure of your own place. Now /

BUNCE

Nah, I'm on it.

GRIFFIN

Paul – I'm tryin' to make an important announcement.

BUNCE

I'm sorry yeah – but my name's down.

GRIFFIN

Well that's news to me – now / the Principal –

BUNCE

Long as you know.

GRIFFIN

Paul can I speak –?!

BUNCE

Yeah sorry, but – I'm with the 'Few'.

GRIFFIN

Right now Paul, your behaviour is showing why you
are most definitely with the 'Many'.

BUNCE

Nah – no way. No way. I'm with the 'Few'.

GRIFFIN

You can't just barge your way through the Narrow-
Gates Paul.

BUNCE

I ain't bargin' nuttin'. What I gotta do that for – I'm
with the Few – my name's down.

GRIFFIN

So you've scribbled it on at the bottom of the list?

BUNCE

Nah I know it – I feel it. This is it for me. I ain't doin'
nuttin' no more – I'm takin' the pills – but I ain't
seein' no doctors no more or nuttin'. I don't need to
see 'em – I got Jesus in my life now, see what I'm
sayin'. He's listenin' yeah – 'cause he's got time. An'
no one's ever got any time to listen to ya – help you
sort out your head –

GRIFFIN

Paul that's / enough.

BUNCE

An' these people are gettin' paid to do it – Doctors,
Shrinks, Social Workers – they're takin' money, but
they don't do nuttin'!

GRIFFIN

Paul!

BUNCE

Nuttin'! Just give it the same ol' questions over an'
over again – an' they ain't even listenin'!

GRIFFIN

Paul have you taken your medication today?

BUNCE

Nah I ain't alright! I ain't takin' that shit no more
neither.

GRIFFIN

Paul I'm hitting the emergency.

BUNCE

Pump you full of pills an' tell you to piss off – they don't listen to ya. You're tryin' to tell them what's in your head but they ain't fuckin' listenin' to ya. Just writing shit down, writing shit down, writing shit down – but they ain't fuckin' listenin'! No one's fuckin' listenin'!

GRIFFIN

Everyone just take it easy.

BUNCE

They're takin' the fuckin' money but they don't do nuttin' for ya. An' I can speak to Jesus twenty-four hours a day, three hundred and sixty-five days a year and he don't aks for nuttin'. He's listenin' to me an' he don't aks for nuttin' – s' how I know – my name's down. My name is down – I'm goin' – (*To Griffin.*) So you can fuck off!

GRIFFIN

(*to Group-member*)

Roger hit the emergency.

BUNCE

You can fuck off 'cause you don't know nuttin'. I'm here every week, I'm tellin' you – my name's down.

Roger tries to navigate a path to the emergency button.

I can tell you now, I spoke to Jesus an' none of you are goin' – none of you. (*Racing for door.*) Get away from me alright. You're fuckin' eviiiiil!

Bunce charges out of the room before Roger can hit the emergency button.

GRIFFIN

'Broad is the way, that leadeth to destruction.' (*To Roger.*) Sit down Roger.

INT. PRAYER ROOM – DAY

A beeper sounds in the blackout. The lights fade up to reveal the Principal standing impatiently alone in the middle of the room, checking his pager.

He fastens the pager back in his belt clip, strolling round the room, browsing the religious paraphernalia, bemused.

A knock on the door.

PRINCIPAL
(*calling*)

Come.

Rilla pops her head round the door.

Ah good – you're here.

RILLA
(*entering*)

Sorry, I'm a bit –

PRINCIPAL

No problem, no problem. (*Pointing to clock.*) Although I do have to be getting on fairly sharpish.

RILLA

Mmm.

PRINCIPAL

So – (*Looking round room.*) This is the place – the Prayer-Room? Never actually been in here before – but understand it's supposed to encourage Cultural Integration –?

RILLA
(*beat*)
What's happening – are we going to be allowed back in the room?

PRINCIPAL
Rilla – I honestly don't know.

RILLA
You're the bloody Principal!

PRINCIPAL
Alright, just – keep your voice down. Well, let's look at the facts /

RILLA
The facts are – you gave us space in this room, we were in here, those fucking animals came in /

PRINCIPAL
Ssshhh. I think /

RILLA
(*lowering volume*)
Those animals came in here and ripped up a Torah – that might not mean anything to you, but to us it's our Holy Book.

PRINCIPAL
Rilla, I think you know very well that I'm aware of that. (*Beat.*) I'm led to believe a few shredded Korans were found scattered around the car park.

RILLA
Nothing to do with us.

PRINCIPAL
Hmmm. I think you've got to understand my position in this.

RILLA
What about our position?!

PRINCIPAL

Rilla, I'm Principal of this college – but I was bending
a few rules to get you in here so quickly.

RILLA

So do it again!

PRINCIPAL

Rilla, that's not how this is going to work – the
Muslims should never have lost Friday in the first
place.

RILLA

And we should have had our own day in the first / place.

PRINCIPAL

Okay, okay, look – I've called a meeting with the heads
of the groups concerned /

RILLA

I wanna be there.

PRINCIPAL

Well as head of the Jewish Society – yes, you will have
to be there.

RILLA

I wanna look in their eyes when they try and spread
their lies.

PRINCIPAL

It's a meeting to reconcile matters – not make them
worse. It's taken me enough to get it to this stage – so
please understand.

RILLA

What about those pigs?

PRINCIPAL

Your attackers? Well, the young man's getting the
backing of the Muslim Council – so it'll be difficult to
do anything there.

RILLA

Ah no, no, no, no, no, / no, no.

PRINCIPAL

The young woman though – doesn't seem to have the
same support, so we should be able to press full
charges there.

RILLA

They should both be hung.

PRINCIPAL

Now Rilla, okay – I didn't hear that. If her previous
record's anything to go by, she could be put away for a
long time.

RILLA

I hope they throw away the key.

PRINCIPAL

(*pointing to clock*)

Which is one commodity that is rarely accorded me –
not even for prayer.

The Principal makes his way to the door.

(*Turning to Rilla.*) Stay if you like – until the next Group
comes in. But don't get into any fights for God's sake.

RILLA

Thanks.

*The Principal opens the door to exit, pausing a second and
turning to face Rilla.*

PRINCIPAL

Rilla – if it means anything to you – I do love your
mother.

RILLA

(*beat*)

I don't want to lose the room.

He nods and exits.

INT. PRAYER ROOM – DAY

In the blackout, some Koranic recitation.

> BROTHER KAZI
> *(voice-over, in blackout)*
> Bismillahir rahmanir rahim. Qul ya ayyuhal kafirun.
> La a'budu ma ta'budun.

Lights up. Brother Kazi is alone, sitting cross-legged on the floor, reciting out loud from the Koran, perched in front of him on a small wooden plinth. He rocks gently back and forth as he follows the text with the index finger of his right hand.

> Wa la antum abiduna ma a'bud. Wa la ana abidum
> ma'abadtum.

A timid knock on the door and Griffin enters cagily – eyeing Brother Kazi.

> GRIFFIN

> Oh –

Brother Kazi maintains his recitation – holding a finger up to Griffin – 'Be with you in a moment.' Griffin takes a little umbrage to this – turning his back.

> BROTHER KAZI
> Wa la antum abiduna ma a'bud. La kum dinukum
> walia din.

Brother Kazi promptly wraps up his recitation –

> Amin. Bismillahir rahmanir rahim.

He runs his hands down his face, blows down the front of his shirt and closes his Koran. He wraps the Holy Book back in its cloth sleeve and stands.

> *(On rising.)* Allah-ho-akbar.

And places the Koran on a high shelf. Griffin watches – furtively transfixed.

> *(To Griffin.)* Here for the meeting – yeah?

86

GRIFFIN

That's right.

BROTHER KAZI

Salaam Bruvver. (*Offering hand.*) Kazi.

GRIFFIN
(*tentative handshake*)

Oh, em – Matthew.

BROTHER KAZI

Good to meet you Maffew.

GRIFFIN

Mmm.

BROTHER KAZI
(*beat*)

Let's hope we can sort all this out.

GRIFFIN

Yes.

BROTHER KAZI

Mean it's no good. End of the day yeah, we's all God's
People innit.

GRIFFIN
(*nodding*)

Mmm.

*Griffin gazes round the room, noticing all the pictures of Christ
covered up.*

BROTHER KAZI

'Cause violence yeah – don't solve nuttin' – is it.

GRIFFIN

Certainly what the Bible says.

BROTHER KAZI

Yeah, the Koran says /

D'you mind – sorry – d'you mind – these pictures –
can we not have them covered –?

BROTHER KAZI
(*looking round room*)
Eh – sorry, yeah, yeah – nah of course.

GRIFFIN
(*uncovering pictures*)
Thank you.

BROTHER KAZI
(*helping*)
Nah, just – I's readin' the Koran innit. Our religion
yeah – you can't show no likeness of no prophets or
nuttin' – s'what we call Haram – ain't good for you.

GRIFFIN
Yes well – I believe this is a meeting, not a prayer-
session.

BROTHER KAZI
(*beat*)
No problem.

*The pair revert to silence for a few moments. A knock on the door
– Rilla sticks her head in the room.*

RILLA
(*spying Griffin, muttering to herself*)
Oh great. (*To Kazi and Griffin.*) The Principal's not
here yet –?

GRIFFIN
So you don't know –?

RILLA
Excuse me –?

GRIFFIN
Thought you might have seen him – on your way here.

RILLA
Yeah right. (*Speaking off.*) D'you think –?

REUBEN
(*emerging*)
Well the meeting ain't out here.

Reuben appears, waltzing into the room – eyeballing Kazi, but Griffin in particular. Rilla follows him in, closing the door.

BROTHER KAZI
(*offering hand to Reuben*)
Salaam Bruvver. Kazi.

REUBEN
(*frosty handshake*)
Shalom.

BROTHER KAZI
(*waving to Rilla*)
Sistah –?

Rilla just nods semi-courteously. Slight pause.

Sorry – Kazi. Didn't catch your names –?

RILLA
Rilla. He's –

REUBEN
Reuben.

BROTHER KAZI
Ma'shallah, ma'shallah – nice names. (*Slight pause.*)
You've met – (*Gesturing to Griffin.*) Maffew yeah –?

GRIFFIN
Yes.

BROTHER KAZI
Right. Right. You guys – used to share – right?

89

REUBEN
(*eyeballing Griffin*)

Mmm.

BROTHER KAZI
Well I just wanna say – that ain't right. From our point
of view yeah – the Muslim Council – I just wanna
make one thing clear /

RILLA
I think we should wait for the Principal.

BROTHER KAZI
Yeah – s'that what everybody thinks –?

Nobody really reacts.

Okay – we wait.

*The small Group stand in awkward silence a little while –
Griffin and Reuben giving each other serious daggers.*

GRIFFIN
(*to Reuben*)

Excuse me –?

Reuben just stares back.

Excuse me – are you staying?

REUBEN
Are you?

GRIFFIN
It was my understanding that this was a meeting
between the heads – I'd like to know what you're
doing here?

REUBEN
(*shrugging*)
That's my understanding.

GRIFFIN

Are you the head of the Jewish Society?

RILLA

It's a shared position – something our religion
encourages.

GRIFFIN

Oh is that right? (*Pointing to board.*) I'm looking at the
board – (*To Reuben.*) I don't see your name.

Reuben crosses to the board, examining it.

REUBEN

Yeah, yeah – you're right.

Reuben grabs a marker, scrawling his name up appropriately.

Are we happy –?

BROTHER KAZI
(*tutting*)

T-t-t-t-t-t.

GRIFFIN
(*to Rilla*)

Is vandalism something that's also encouraged?

Rilla just scowls back. The Principal enters breezily.

PRINCIPAL

Apologies everyone – right up against it today.

GRIFFIN

Hello Principal.

PRINCIPAL

Yes, yes eh – you've all met, I take it –?

BROTHER KAZI

We have yeah.

PRINCIPAL

Okay – let's grab some seats – not waiting on anyone
else, are we?

GRIFFIN

No – but I would like some clarification on the
personnel who were supposed to be attending this
meeting.

RILLA

I told you.

GRIFFIN

It was my understanding that this was intended as a
meeting between the Heads of the three main religious
Groups.

RILLA
(*to Principal*)
We're Joint-Heads.

PRINCIPAL

You –? Sorry, bear with me – (*Beat.*) Okay – yes, this is
a meeting between the Heads of the eh, the three main
religious Groups, yes. (*Beat.*) So –?

RILLA
(*pointing to Griffin*)
He is saying that Reuben should not be here /

GRIFFIN

He shouldn't /

REUBEN

Get off /

RILLA

But I've already told them – we're Joint-Heads.

PRINCIPAL

Joint-Heads?

RILLA

That's right – there's only two of us.

PRINCIPAL
(*to Reuben*)

Joint-Heads?

REUBEN

That's right, sir.

PRINCIPAL

Okay, okay – (*To Kazi and Griffin.*) And this is a problem –?

GRIFFIN

It just seems very convenient.

PRINCIPAL

Hmmm – (*To Kazi.*) Mister . . . Kafi?

BROTHER KAZI

Kazi.

PRINCIPAL

Apologies – Kazi – hectic day. Yes – your position is –?

BROTHER KAZI

You's the Chairman.

PRINCIPAL

Okay – (*Eyes up Reuben.*) There's only two of you – I don't see any reason to object.

GRIFFIN
(*aside*)

Surprise.

PRINCIPAL

Don't believe it's the foot we should be stepping off on.

RILLA

Exactly.

PRINCIPAL
(*to Kazi and Griffin*)
Gentlemen – okay –? (*Motioning to chairs.*) So – shall
we? Time I'm afraid is never kind to me.

They sit.

So – I'd like to start by saying a sincere thank you to
you all for coming here today and showing a – a joint
determination to sort out what I'm sure we all agree
was an unfortunate incident.

GRIFFIN
It was. But I think it's important to point out, that we
had no part in this.

BROTHER KAZI
I think /

PRINCIPAL
But you have an interest in the room –? And you
accept that there's some conflict in the scheduling –?

GRIFFIN
We have an interest in the room – yes. But we have
never been party to any conflict.

RILLA
You do nothing but!

BROTHER KAZI
I think /

PRINCIPAL
Alright, okay – this meeting is not about the assignation
or apportioning of guilt or blame. With the help of –
(*Motioning to Kazi.*) Mister eh – the Muslim Council –
and the police, that job is already being taken care of.
(*To Rilla.*) The young man has been suspended /

RILLA
He was the bloody perpetrator.

94

PRINCIPAL

Rilla –

BROTHER KAZI

Sistah, he didn't know 'bout no changes.

RILLA

And that makes it alright for him to barge in on us –
while we're praying?

BROTHER KAZI

Looking at the big-picture yeah, it looks kinda wrong –
I can see that. But in the little picture – he didn't know.

PRINCIPAL

Rilla I think /

RILLA

(*to Principal*)

And you believe that?

PRINCIPAL

The young girl, Jade Williams, has been charged and
pleaded guilty and, as suspected, had quite an
extensive previous. It's never good to see any of your
students going to prison – particularly those from a,
from a less privileged background – but neither is it
acceptable to attack fellow-students – especially in
what is supposed to be a place of worship. So, please –
let's try not to get bogged down in the who's and
why's of it all. Let's stick to the task at hand and see if
we can't come to some kind of workable arrangement,
whereby all parties feel they are getting as much use
out of the College's facilities as we can offer. Okay –?

REUBEN

(*beat*)

Fine.

PRINCIPAL

Thank you. So situation at present is – correct me if
I'm wrong – (*To Griffin.*) Your people have two days –?

95

GRIFFIN

Correct.

PRINCIPAL
(*to Kazi*)
Your people have one day –?

BROTHER KAZI

S'right.

PRINCIPAL
(*to Reuben and Rilla*)
And you people have half a day?

RILLA

Well we haven't yet.

PRINCIPAL
But that is the, eh – the schedule as it stands –?

GRIFFIN

Seems fine to me.

BROTHER KAZI
But we've lost half a day – (*To Principal.*) They both
gained half.

PRINCIPAL

Okay, okay /

RILLA
We should have a full day.

GRIFFIN
For only two of you?

REUBEN
Difference should that / make?

PRINCIPAL
Alright, okay, the solution is usually staring you right
in the face and if we give it a chance it might present
itself. (*To Griffin.*) You have two days –?

GRIFFIN

And always have.

PRINCIPAL

But you used to share a half-day with eh – (*Thumbing
Rilla and Reuben.*) With this lot.

GRIFFIN

It was a convenient arrangement to a point /

RILLA

For you maybe.

GRIFFIN
(*to Rilla*)

Sorry – can I talk –? (*To Principal.*) If I'm going to be
interrupted every two seconds –

PRINCIPAL

No, no – let's try and maintain some order – Rilla –
(*To Griffin.*) Sorry, you were saying –?

GRIFFIN

Thank you. It was convenient because it was only her.
It's certainly impractical – from our point of view
anyway – to share with any more than one.

PRINCIPAL

Okay, okay – so you would not favour rekindling that
arrangement with the eh, with the Muslims?

GRIFFIN

Absolutely not – (*To Kazi.*) No offence.

BROTHER KAZI

No problem. It's not somethin' that I could see
workin'.

PRINCIPAL

Why's that –?

BROTHER KAZI

There's too many impracticalities innit – numbers for
a start.

PRINCIPAL

I see.

BROTHER KAZI

Just one day ain't enough for us. We can't turn people
away – but too many peoples in the room – Health 'n'
Safety ain't gonna like that.

PRINCIPAL

No, no – they wouldn't.

REUBEN

Why how many of you is there?

BROTHER KAZI

There's over a billion Muslims in the world Bruvver –
fastest growin' religion in the planet.

RILLA

Some people'll believe anything.

BROTHER KAZI

Excuse me –?

GRIFFIN

There's well over a billion Christians.

PRINCIPAL

Okay, okay – are you people saying that you are
opposed to any kind of sharing?

The Group just squirm uneasily.

GRIFFIN
(*beat*)

I don't see how it's workable from our point of view.

BROTHER KAZI

I will say this – in the history of Islam yeah, it has been

shown, that we are able to live in harmony with those
of a different religious belief.

PRINCIPAL
So you see sharing as an option?

BROTHER KAZI
Well – no. Not in this instance.

RILLA
(*to Kazi*)
No I'm sorry, excuse me – you have a history of 'living
in harmony' with other religions?

BROTHER KAZI
S'right – Islam says if people wanna worship their own
God – let 'em do it. No matter what.

RILLA
Mmm, yeah, sure – as long as you pay something
like triple the taxes, bow when a Muslim passes you
in the street, and generally live life as a third-class
citizen, shouting 'Muslims are great' every ten
minutes.

BROTHER KAZI
Nah – that ain't right.

PRINCIPAL
Okay now – just /

RILLA
Oh, really –? 'Al-Dhimmi' mean anything to you –?

BROTHER KAZI
I know Al-Dhimmi.

PRINCIPAL
Okay let's /

RILLA
'Cause that is exactly the prototype-Apartheid system

99

that your 'harmonious' people made us and other
religions live under.

PRINCIPAL

Rilla, that's enough.

GRIFFIN

We are no party to / conflict.

BROTHER KAZI

Nah, nah, nah, nah, nah – get your facts right, yeah,
get your facts right. I'll tell you right now yeah, that in
Muslim-Spain the Jews were given high positions –
I'm talkin' Top Jobs, the Government, everythin'
yeah.

REUBEN

So what's changed?

BROTHER KAZI

Before the Muslims yeah, the Jews was gettin' well
persecuted by the Vandals /

REUBEN

Oh c'mon.

BROTHER KAZI
(*pointing to Griffin*)

He said it earlier.

GRIFFIN

Said what –?!

BROTHER KAZI

Don't matter. (*To Rilla.*) Then it was the Christians –
been them that's persecuting you – ain't / us.

GRIFFIN

Excuse me?!

BROTHER KAZI

S'true.

GRIFFIN

How dare you say / that?

PRINCIPAL

Okay, I think that's /

BROTHER KAZI

Hitler weren't no Muslim.

GRIFFIN

He was a bloody Catholic!

REUBEN

Isn't that Christian?

GRIFFIN

You're not even supposed to / be here.

PRINCIPAL

Can we all just /

RILLA

Like to get rid of us all wouldn't you /?

The door slowly creaks open – hushing the Group. They watch with bated breath, as the door seems to take an eternity to swing fully open – to finally reveal Fiz, standing silently, fixing Reuben with a horrid glare.

BROTHER KAZI

Bruvver –?

Fiz remains silent.

PRINCIPAL

You're suspended, aren't you?

Fiz remains silent – eyes piercing into Reuben.

Excuse me –? (*To Kazi.*) What's his name –?

BROTHER KAZI

Bruvver Hafiz. (*To Fiz.*) Bruvver – we still in the meeting yeah – (*Making phone gesture.*) I'll bell you innit.

Fiz remains silent, eyes fixed on Reuben.

PRINCIPAL
Hafiz – you do understand the terms of your
suspension? It's not just your classes – you're
suspended from the College grounds full-stop. I'm
sorry but I have to ask you to leave.

Fiz remains silent, eyes fixed on Reuben.

Hafiz – don't make this any worse for yourself.

BROTHER KAZI
Bruvver – we can talk later alright?

Fiz remains silent, eyes fixed on Reuben.

REUBEN
(*beat*)
What? (*Fiz just stares.*) If you wanna say somethin' to
me, say it. (*Fiz just stares.*) C'mon then. Say it. (*Fiz just
stares.*) Say it! What've you got to say – say it!

RILLA
Reuben –

REUBEN
No, no – who does he think I am? He's not gonna
intimidate me. Look at him – he's a joke. (*To Fiz.*)
Think you've gotta cause to fight for? Think you, think
you – well say somethin'. (*Fiz just stares.*) C'mon I'm
here – what's your problem?

Fiz just stares at Reuben.

PRINCIPAL
I think we need Security in here.

BROTHER KAZI
Bruvver – this ain't gonna help you none if you don't
get outta here.

Fiz just stares at Reuben.

REUBEN

What? What?! You gonna kill me or somethin' – that
it?

FIZ
(*beat*)

Yeah.

The Group become very rigid, Fiz brooding before them.

(*Slight pause.*) She was gonna be good. (*Beat.*) A
good Muslim. She was. (*Beat.*) Who ain't done bad
shit in their time? She done some bad shit yeah – but
who ain't – see? She weren't like that no more. She
weren't like that. (*Beat.*) I met her yeah, she didn't
know nuttin' 'bout God or shit. She's just like hanging
around an' shit, outside her flats, nuttin' to do –
(*To Brother Kazi.*) You know what's it like –?

BROTHER KAZI

Yeah Bruvver – alright – just take it easy.

FIZ

She ain't got no Dad, her Mum ain't interested in shit
but liquor – what she got? Nuttin'. 'Course she's
gonna get into bad shit – half the fuckin' kids in this
country doin' the same – more than half – innit – (*To
Kazi.*) Innit –? That's what you gotta do to survive –
do that bad shit. You don't do that, you ain't got shit.
An' everybody's got shit but you ain't got none – what
you gonna do?!

BROTHER KAZI

Easy bruvver.

FIZ

You gonna do bad shit – that's what you gonna do. But
I told her she didn't need that no more. All that bad
shit – she didn't need it no more – 'cause she got Allah
innit – (*To Kazi.*) Innit –? She's gonna take her

Shahada an' everythin'. I's gonna marry d'at girl –
(*Beat.*) S'what I told her. She take her Shahada, we get
married, that'd be it kool – we don't need to worry
'bout nuttin' no more. Ain't nobody could say nuttin'
to us no more – we'd be kool. We'd be kool. But that
ain't happenin' no more.

Fiz pulls out a handgun from his pocket – the Group cower.

BROTHER KAZI

Bruvver nah – this ain't the way – this ain't the way.
Put the gun down Bruvver – put it down.

FIZ

She's gone. An' I don't know who she gonna be when
she come out.

Fiz points the gun on Reuben.

REUBEN

For God's sake – take it easy.

FIZ

You lookin' for him now. You lookin' for God?! You?!
(*Darting forward.*) What'd I say to you – huh?! What'd
I say?

REUBEN

I dunno – what'd you say?!

FIZ

I told you don't touch her – what'd I say? I told you
I's gonna kill you if you / touched her.

RILLA

She attacked me, / please!

GRIFFIN

I wasn't there!

BROTHER KAZI

Bruvver – this ain't you, c'mon. This ain't you.

Now I can't touch her. (*Aiming at Reuben.*) You fuckin'
Kafir /

REUBEN

No! Please mate no!

BROTHER KAZI

Bruvver don't do it!

RILLA

Leave us alone /

GRIFFIN

Jesus have mercy /

*The door bursts open – Bunce standing in the doorway,
buncing.*

BUNCE

Lookin' for Matthew –? (*Beat.*) S'goin' on –?

*The scene is frozen for a moment – except of course for Bunce's
buncing – in a tableau.*

PRINCIPAL

Get him!

Fiz is rushed by Brother Kazi, Reuben and the Principal.

REUBEN
(*rushing Fiz*)

You fuckin' prick!

*As the Group swarm round Fiz – BANG – the gun goes off.
Bunce stops buncing for the first time.*

BROTHER KAZI
(*holding down Fiz*)

We got him.

PRINCIPAL
(*holding gun*)

Everyone alright –?

RILLA

Fine /

REUBEN

Yeah /

GRIFFIN
(*frantically checking*)
I can't feel anything.

PRINCIPAL
Everyone –? (*Motioning.*) Rilla – the emergency.

Rilla moves for the emergency button. Bunce is dumbfounded by his lack of bunce.

BUNCE
Fuckin' 'ell! (*Checking himself over.*) Shit – look at that – I'm alright! (*Pointing to gun.*) S'that thing real?

A pool of red blood oozes across Bunce's shirt – everyone notices.

GRIFFIN
(*beat*)

Paul –?

BUNCE
(*looking at blood*)
Shit – (*Looking to Griffin.*) Sorry –

Bunce collapses to the ground in a heap.

Students come piling in. The emergency bell rings. Screams are heard. Mouths are agape. The lights fade slowly.

RILLA
(*wailing*)
Oh God! Oh God!

Blackout.

Music plays out.

The End.